THE EPISTLES OF PAUL
TO THE THESSALONIANS

An Exposition

THE EPISTLES
OF PAUL
TO THE
THESSALONIANS

An Exposition

by
CHARLES R. ERDMAN

PREFACE BY EARL F. ZEIGLER

THE WESTMINSTER PRESS
PHILADELPHIA

Third printing, 1975

Published by The Westminster Press®
Philadelphia, Pennsylvania

PRINTED IN THE UNITED STATES OF AMERICA

PREFACE

In about twenty minutes a person can complete a reading, aloud, of the text of the two oldest books in the New Testament. These are the First and Second Letters to the Thessalonians. The writer was the apostle Paul, perhaps in collaboration with Silas and Timothy. The date of the letters was around A.D. 50, and the city from which they were written was Corinth.

Incidentally, reading Paul's letters aloud is a good habit to acquire. He probably dictated them in a speaking voice, and certainly when the letters reached their destination they were read *aloud* to the church members who met in homes for worship. (There were no Christian church edifices as such in those days.) And we can be certain that there were no duplicating machines to run off copies of Paul's letters to distribute to the congregation. In time his letters were "duplicated" by the slow process of hand copying. So, by reading the letters aloud something of the sound and cadence of Paul's voice can be transmitted to the twentieth-century reader. But whether aloud or in silence, the letters of Paul are "prescribed" reading for everyone who is concerned about his own spiritual enlightenment and growth.

All Christians need some kind of help in studying the Bible. This volume on I and II Thessalonians is one kind of study help—and a very present help at that. The writer of the book was Dr. Charles R. Erdman, sometime professor of practical theology in Princeton Seminary. He was also a pastor of three different thriving churches in Philadelphia and Princeton. The church at large was enriched by his leadership in the foreign mission board, and in many other services. He was also a moderator of the Presbyterian Church in the U.S.A. His gifts as a Biblical expositor and interpreter are second to none. He has a way of stating things clearly, aptly, forcefully but fairly, and with evangelistic passion. His objectivity in regard to Biblical material was perfectly related to his convictions on the essential teachings of Scripture.

In his exposition of I and II Thessalonians, Dr. Erdman has to explain the references to the Second Coming of Christ which had caused so much agitation and concern among the members of the Thessalonian church. Obviously, the Second Coming as a doctrine still "agitates and concerns" millions of Christians. In some churches it is a divisive doctrine. The manner in which Dr. Erdman comments on matters of such significance as this provides the present-day student of God's Word with most helpful guidance.

This study of I and II Thessalonians gives students of many varieties—Sunday school teachers, pastors, college and seminary students, young people in the churches, and other lay men and women—a way to have fellowship with believers in the early church in their life and work. The membership consisted of converted Jews, and "a great many of the devout Greeks and not a few of the leading women" (Acts 17:4). It is a remarkable testimony to the power of the Holy Spirit that within a few weeks (or months at the most) orthodox Jews, idol worshipers, inquiring Gentiles, and society women were consolidated into a fellowship of faith and worship and good works and godly living—the Christian church.

If the Holy Spirit could do that in the first century, who are we to disbelieve in his power to make disciples of the nations in this century?

EARL F. ZEIGLER

FOREWORD

These two brief letters are of profound interest to all who are seeking to solve the practical problems of life, or looking for light in the spheres of the spiritual and the divine. They make their most arresting appeal, however, to persons who are concerned with the evangelization of the world, for these are the earliest missionary documents extant. They embody the spirit and message of primitive Christianity. By them is disclosed the secret of the present transforming power of Christ. In them is found the inspiring prediction of the future universal triumph of his cause.

INTRODUCTION

THE CITY OF THESSALONICA

Thessalonica was built on the site of the ancient town of Therma, or Therme. The latter name was derived from the warm mineral springs (*thermae*) which still exist in the region. The new city seems to have been founded about the year 315 B.C. by the Macedonian king, Cassander. He concentrated the populations of several neighboring towns and villages and renamed the place Thessalonica in honor of his wife, who was a daughter of Philip II, king of Macedon, and sister of Alexander the Great.

The place grew rapidly in size and wealth, due in large measure to the rich surrounding plains and to its superb natural harbor. Therefore, when Macedonia was conquered by the Romans in 168 B.C., Thessalonica was made the capital of one of its four divisions. Then, in 146 B.C., when the country was converted into a Roman province, it became the residence of the governor and practically the provincial capital.

Under the government of Rome the city continued to advance in prosperity. It stood on the inmost bay of the Thermaic Gulf. Through the city ran the great Via Egnatia, or Egnatian highway. Consequently Thessalonica became one of the most important commercial centers between the Adriatic and the Hellespont. Thus Cicero could speak of the Thessalonians as "placed in the lap of the Empire," and in this city, in 58 B.C., he spent a part of his exile.

In the First Civil War, between the forces of Caesar and Pompey, 49 B.C., Thessalonica was on the side of Pompey; but in the Second Civil War, in 42 B.C., it stood on the side of Antony and Octavian. This loyalty was rewarded by the city's being given the status and privilege of a "free city." Therefore, the citizens were given the right of holding their assembly and of appointing their own magistrates. The latter were known as "rulers of the city," of "politarchs," a term thus used with absolute accuracy by Luke in recording the visit of Paul to Thessalonica. Thus, in contrast with the neighboring city of Philippi, which was a Roman "colony," Thessalonica was essentially Greek in its character, and so it has ever continued to be. In the days of Paul it contained a mixed population of native Greeks, Roman colonists, Orientals, and a large settlement of Jews. In the early Christian centuries the city became of ever greater prominence and for a time, before the rise of Constantinople, was regarded as the possible future capital of the world.

In later Roman history the city was a bulwark against the invasions of the Goths. In the Middle Ages it was captured by the Saracens, A.D. 904, by the Normans in A.D. 1185, and by the Turks in A.D. 1430. During the World War, 1914–1918, under its modern name of Saloniki, or Salonika, it was the base of important military operations, and was at that time, next to Constantinople, the chief city of European Turkey.

Now Greek influence is again supreme; so that "on the whole, Salonika may be said still to be what it has been for more than twenty centuries—a center of Hellenic influence and civilization." Of all the cities of the ancient world, connected with the life and labors of the apostle Paul, none, with the single exception of Rome, has so maintained its character and importance down to the present day as has Salonika.

THE THESSALONIAN CHURCH

The existence of a church in this flourishing commercial and political center was due to the missionary efforts of Paul. As to the establishment and the character of this church, many details are found recorded by Luke in Acts (ch. 17), and many others are provided by references in the two epistles to the Thessalonians which have come from the pen of the apostle Paul. It thus appears that on his second missionary journey, Paul crossed from Asia to Europe, and first undertook work in Philippi, where he was beaten and imprisoned but where he was able to organize a devoted and flourishing church. Leaving this Roman colony he followed the Egnatian Road a hundred miles southwest, passing through Amphipolis and Apollonia, to the larger and more important city of Thessalonica.

There he found a synagogue of the Jews, where for three successive Sabbaths he proclaimed the gospel. He appealed to the Old Testament Scriptures, proving by exposition and quotation that the promised Messiah was "to suffer, and to rise again from the dead," and affirming that "this Jesus," whom he preached, had fulfilled all these predictions and was indeed the Messiah.

There was also another phase of truth made prominent in this preaching of Paul. From the charge brought against him of "saying that there is another king, one Jesus," and from the main teachings of his two letters later addressed to the Thessalonian church, it is evident that Paul emphasized the doctrine of the Kingdom, as set forth by Jesus, and of the final establishment of this Kingdom by the personal appearing of the risen and exalted King.

The result of this preaching was the conversion of "some" Jews; of "devout Greeks," or Gentile proselytes to the Jewish faith, "a great multitude"; and of "not a few" women of high social position. In addition to these Jewish converts, however, the First Epistle makes it evident that there were still larger numbers of converts from heathenism. (I Thess. 1:9; 2:14.) These and other references in the epistle indicate that Paul must have remained in Thessalonica longer than the "three sabbath days" specified by Luke in his account. It would seem that when only a comparatively few Jews of the synagogue "were persuaded, and consorted with Paul," he turned directly to the Gentiles, establishing a new center in the city, and continuing his mission for a number of weeks, possibly even of months. Indications of such a longer period are found in the fact that twice during his stay in Thessalonica, Paul received gifts from his friends in Philippi, one hundred miles distant, and in the facts that he established himself in his trade of tentmaking and further that he found time not only for public preaching but also for visitation from house to house.

It was for Paul and his companions a time of strenuous work and faithful testimony. They rebuked idolatry, warned against impurity, predicted the coming wrath of God and the saving power of Christ. They instructed Christians in the necessity of holy living and comforted them by the assurance of the return of Christ and their "gathering together unto him."

This ministry was attended by great success. Believers rapidly increased in numbers. They were endowed with the gifts of the Holy Spirit; they bore testimony by consecrated lives to the power of God; and they were strong to endure opposition, persecution, and reproach for the sake of Christ.

The very success of the mission aroused the envy and the hostility of the unbelieving Jews. They stirred up the dregs of the city populace, gathered a mob, and began "assaulting the house of Jason," where the missionaries probably were lodging. Not finding them, they seized Jason and certain other converts and dragged them before the magistrates, accusing them of harboring men who had disturbed the peace of the world, who acted "contrary to the decrees of Cæsar" and claimed allegiance to a rival king. As no evidence of lawless practices was presented against Jason and his companions, they were bound over to keep the peace and were released. Fearing further disorder and peril, the friends of Paul sent him and Silas by night to Berea. There his reception was kindly and his work was successful, until the news of his success reached the Jews of

Thessalonica, who hastened to Berea, raised a disturbance, and made it necessary for Paul to leave for Athens. In Thessalonica, however, Paul had been able to establish a strong and vigorous church. Some years must have passed before he was able to revisit his converts in that Macedonian city. Yet they were constantly in his mind. His two epistles to the Thessalonians are monuments to his friendship and affection. Nor were his labors in vain. For centuries Thessalonica remained a stronghold of Christianity and was known as "the Orthodox City." The chief claim to distinction for either this city or this church is based upon no achievement of its citizens or its Christian converts, but upon the fact that to a group of believers in Thessalonica two brief immortal letters were addressed by the missionary apostle, Paul.

The Occasion of the Epistles

In The Acts the historian makes no mention of the causes which led Paul to write his letters to the Thessalonian church. The letters themselves, however, contain numerous references which make plain his reasons for writing; and certain historical statements of The Acts make clearer the circumstances under which the letters were composed.

After leaving Berea, Paul had journeyed to Athens. He was still solicitous of his friends in Thessalonica. He gladly would have revisited them, but circumstances forbade. Therefore, from Athens, he dispatched Timothy, his beloved companion, to bear his greetings to the Thessalonian church and to learn its condition. After the departure of Timothy, Paul passed on to Corinth. Here he made his home with Aquila and Priscilla, and supported himself by working at his trade as a tentmaker. Paul discoursed every Sabbath in the synagogue, but his efforts were bitterly opposed by the Jews. Paul was discouraged. However, the arrival of Silas and Timothy from Macedonia and a vision of his divine Lord gave Paul new cheer and he continued his work in Corinth for eighteen months. The arrival of Timothy and the report he brought from the Thessalonian church were the immediate reasons for Paul's First Epistle to this church.

The report in the main was favorable, even joyous. The Thessalonians had been found constant in their faith and love. They were affectionately devoted to Paul and his companions, deeply concerned for his welfare, and eagerly hoping for his return. They had bravely endured persecution. Their consistent Christian character had been widely reported. They were steadfastly expecting the coming of Christ.

Nevertheless, there was much in the tidings brought by Timothy which occasioned Paul deep concern. First of all, it was learned that since his departure, only a few months previously, serious insinuations against the ministry and character of Paul had been circulated by his enemies. The authors of these calumnies seem to have been unbelieving Jews. The substance of these accusations was to the effect that Paul was a teacher of error and had no divine message to proclaim, that he was inspired only by selfish and mercenary motives, that his influence was immoral, that he had used false pretenses to conceal his greed, and that all this was proved by the fact that Paul had not returned to revisit his converts in their need.

That they were in need was manifest, for, in the second place, it was reported by Timothy that the Thessalonian Christians were suffering from bitter persecution. Their enemies were not content with attacking the character of the apostle. They were threatening the property and the persons of the converts. They were attempting to turn them from their faith, not only by slandering Paul, but by offering insult and violence to all who were loyal to his gospel.

In the third place, Paul learned that the Thessalonian Christians were not free from the temptations to immoral practices to which all members of heathen communities were exposed. That they were guilty of serious fault is not declared, but it is evident that their peril was real.

Furthermore, certain doctrinal difficulties were brought to the attention of the apostle. These related to the return of Christ. Paul had taught that this event might occur in his own lifetime or in that of his converts. He never asserted that it would. The time was uncertain. All should live in expectation and in hope. Since Paul had left Thessalonica certain members of the church had died. Their friends feared that these loved ones might not share in the glorious experiences of those who would be alive at the appearing of the Lord.

Then, too, there was the question as to the time of this appearing. Some Christians seemed to be living in feverish anticipation of its imminence, while others were tempted to fall into the indifference and carelessness of unbelievers who had no expectation of the predicted event.

Last of all, there was reported a certain laxity of discipline and a need of more respect and regard for those who held positions of leadership and authority in the infant church.

To meet all these difficulties related to him by Timothy, it is evident that Paul eagerly desired to return to Thessalonica. This was impossible. Therefore, he composed his First Epistle and dispatched it by the hand of a special messenger or a friend.

Possibly the same person, a few months later, brought back the news which led Paul to compose his Second Epistle. Conditions in the church were not much changed. The faith and love of the Thessalonians were still abounding, and their heroic patience was being maintained amid increasing persecution. However, their feverish expectation of the return of Christ had increased. It seems to have been incited by some prediction or utterance or letter purported to have come from Paul. Possibly there had been in this regard some serious misinterpretation of his

First Epistle. The belief existed that "the day of the Lord" was "just at hand" or had actually come. The result was a condition of disorder in the church. Many of its members forsook their daily tasks. They lived in idleness. They supposed that further industry was unnecessary as the end of the age was so near. Therefore, to encourage them in their sufferings, to steady them in their expectations, and to correct their conduct, Paul composed his Second Epistle to the Thessalonians.

THE CONTENTS

The substance of the two brief epistles to the Thessalonians corresponds naturally to the conditions which called them into being. These epistles are not speculative discussions of religious themes, but practical solutions of pressing problems. They are not intended to set forth Christian dogmas but to inspire right conduct. The only doctrine presented is that of the Second Coming of Christ; yet even this important truth is not exhaustively reviewed. It is only introduced to correct one or two misconceptions and to form the basis for practical exhortations to hopefulness, to watchfulness, and to orderly, industrious living.

The letters are in the truest sense "personal" and "occasional," yet for this very reason they contain statements difficult to interpret. Paul takes for granted that the Thessalonians have in mind teachings which have been given previously and that they are expecting answers to questions not repeated in the letters. Passages which must have been plain to the persons addressed are puzzling to readers of the present day.

Epistles so informal cannot be expected to follow any very definite plan. However, it is not difficult to trace a distinct order and progress of thought.

In the case of the First Epistle, it may be divided quite naturally into two parts. The first, comprising three chap-

ters, is essentially "personal." The second, containing the
last two chapters, may be termed "practical" or "ethical,"
because it consists largely of explicit exhortations to consistent Christian life.

The letter opens with a salutation, which in substance
also appears in the later epistles of Paul. Here, however,
he unites with his own name those of his beloved companions, Silvanus, or Silas, and Timothy. He then expresses
gratitude for the spiritual graces of the Thessalonians, for
their "work of faith and labor of love and patience of
hope." He is thankful for the knowledge of the great success in which his mission in Thessalonica has resulted.
This success is due to the power and assurance which attended his preaching and to the eagerness with which the
truth was received. The sincerity of the Thessalonians'
conversion has been attested by consistent and exemplary
lives. Their influence has been extended throughout Macedonia and Achaia by others who have reported the nature
of Paul's ministry and how the Thessalonians have turned
from idols and are awaiting the return of the risen Savior.
(Ch. 1.)

By the way in which he has voiced his thankfulness Paul
has already gone far toward answering the slanders which
seem to have been circulated concerning the nature of his
ministry among the Thessalonians. However, he proceeds
to remind his readers more in detail as to the character of
his ministry. They themselves can bear witness to the
boldness of his preaching, to the absolute sincerity and
unselfishness of his motives, to his tenderness and self-
sacrifice, to the purity of his life, to the affection and encouragement of his fatherly entreaties. (Ch. 2:1-12.)

Paul, furthermore, unites with his readers in thankful
remembrance of the reception which they had given to the
ministry he has just described. They had welcomed his
message as being the very "word of God." This message
had proved to be a vital power in the lives of those who
believed. They had shown the genuineness of their faith

by the steadfastness with which they had endured persecution at the hands of their fellow countrymen. In this they "became imitators of the churches" in Judea that suffered the same things at the hands of the Jews. It is the Jews who have been the determined opponents of the gospel. They killed the Lord and his messengers. They forbade Paul to preach to the Gentiles. Their sins are multiplying, but their judgment is sure. (Vs. 13-16.)

In defense against the charge that he has deserted his converts in Thessalonica, Paul declares that from the time he left them he has been eager to see them. Twice he has tried to come, but has been prevented. Instead of failing in his affection for them he regards them as his glory and his joy. Therefore, when able to endure the separation no longer, he sent Timothy to strengthen their faith and to encourage them to endure the persecution which Paul had warned them to expect. He was even fearful lest amid their sufferings they might possibly have been beguiled from their faith and his work in Thessalonica might have been in vain. (Chs. 2:17 to 3:5.)

The joyful news which Timothy brought of their faith and love and of their personal affection for Paul has given him comfort and new life. Indeed, words fail to express his joy and gratitude as he continually prays that he may be allowed to revisit them and to aid in perfecting their faith. (Ch. 3:6-10.)

In fervent petition Paul requests that this reunion may be granted and that in any case their love may be increased and that their hearts may be established in holiness in view of the approaching return of the Lord. (Vs. 11-13.)

The second portion of the First Epistle (chs. 4; 5) deals with certain practical problems, which, even more than Paul's need of personal defense, were probably the real occasion of the epistle.

First of all, it was necessary to warn his readers of the peril of impurity. He does so tactfully, beginning with the assurance that their manner of life is now pleasing to God.

Yet he does not withhold his warning. They had not fallen, but they were surrounded by temptations. They needed to be reminded of their peril, and to be assured that they had been called to a life of holiness and that to sin is not merely to offend man but to defy God. (Ch. 4:1-8.)

Paul next exhorts his readers to brotherly love and to industry. The latter exhortation may indicate that some had forsaken their daily tasks, either because they were willing to depend upon the charity of others or possibly because of a feverish expectation of an immediate return of the Lord. (Vs. 9-12.)

In any event, Paul here introduces valuable instructions as to the doctrine of the Second Advent. He does so, however, with the practical purpose of giving comfort and encouragement. He touches upon two points concerning the Lord's return:

First, he gives assurance in reference to the dead—that their relation to the risen Christ is such that their resurrection is certain; that instead of their failing to share in the glory of the Advent they will be the first to experience it. "The dead in Christ shall rise first," then the living "shall together with them be caught up in the clouds, to meet the Lord in the air." (Vs. 13-18.)

Secondly, as to the time of the Lord's return, Paul has given previous instruction. The day will come upon unbelievers as a sudden surprise. Those who trust in Christ are not thus to be overtaken. They must "watch and be sober." They have nothing to fear. The coming of Christ will be but the completion of their salvation, whether at his appearing they are living or dead. (Ch. 5:1-11.)

Exhortations are added relative to the corporate life of the church and the personal life of individual believers (vs. 12-22); and the epistle closes with a prayer for the sanctification of the readers, with a command about the reading of the letter, and with a brief benediction (vs. 23-28).

The Second Epistle moves in much the same sphere of thought as does the first, and meets conditions not greatly changed. It may be studied in three general divisions. The first consists of a salutation, a thanksgiving, and a prayer. (Ch. 1.) The second gives instructions concerning the return of Christ. (Ch. 2:1-12.) The third includes thanksgiving and prayers, but more particularly contains exhortations concerning those who are living disorderly lives. (Chs. 2:13 to 3:18.) All three are related in substance to the doctrine of the Lord's return. The first concerns the coming of Christ and the tribulation; the second, the coming of Christ and the man of sin; the third, the coming of Christ and present duty. The first contains "consolation"; the second, "instruction"; the third, "exhortation."

The epistle opens with a salutation, in which Paul again unites with his own name those of his companions, Silvanus and Timothy. Together they send their greetings to the church of the Thessalonians. (Ch. 1:1-2.)

Paul gives thanks for the spiritual state of the Thessalonians, for their increasing faith and love, and particularly for their patient endurance of persecution. This persecution, which evidently is growing more severe, must not make them fear that God has forgotten them. On the contrary, as God is just, their faithful endurance is a pledge of their glorious deliverance "at the revelation of the Lord Jesus from heaven." That day of their vindication will be the day of the destruction of their enemies who have not obeyed the gospel of Christ. (Vs. 3-10.)

Prayer is added that they may be counted worthy of their calling and may be spiritually perfected, to the glory both of the Savior and of themselves. (Vs. 11-12.)

Concerning the return of Christ there was need of instruction. The belief that the day was "just at hand" had been strengthened by false prophecy, or by perverting the teaching of Paul, or by a forged letter purporting to have come from him. He assures his readers that the day will not come until there has been first a great apostasy and "the man of sin" has been revealed. This revelation is being restrained for the present. When the restrainer is "taken out of the way" then "the lawless one" will appear, but will be destroyed, together with his deluded followers, by the coming of Christ. (Ch. 2:1-12.)

Paul returns thanks that his readers are to be delivered from such a doom and are destined to share the glory of Christ. Therefore he exhorts them to "stand fast," and he prays that they may be comforted, and may be established "in every good work and word." (Vs. 13-17.)

Having repeatedly prayed for his readers, Paul now requests that they will pray for him. He expresses confidence in the faithfulness of God and in the obedience of his readers, for whom he again asks that their hearts may abound in "the love of God" and "the patience of Christ." (Ch. 3:1-5.)

He now reaches one of the main purposes of the letter as he deals with those who are walking "disorderly." Evidently, moved by feverish expectation of the return of Christ, many were neglecting their daily tasks. Such conduct is contrary to the teaching and example and explicit command of Paul. The offenders must change their course and earn their own bread. Their fellow Christians must not countenance their conduct even while regarding them still with brotherly love. (Vs. 6-15.)

The letter closes with a prayer for peace, with Paul's autograph salutation, and with a familiar benediction. (Vs. 16-18.)

THE VALUE OF THE EPISTLES

Brief and informal as these letters are, they have been regarded rightfully as a priceless heritage of the Christian church. Any message from Paul is precious. As truly authentic it is accepted as apostolic, authoritative, inspired.

These letters do not attain the mystic heights of The Epistle of Paul to the Ephesians; they do not display the logical skill of The Epistle of Paul to the Romans; but they do possess a value which in some elements is unique.

First of all, they give a fascinating portrait of Paul as a missionary, a consoler, and a prophet. Quite as truly as in The Epistle of Paul to the Philippians and in The Second Epistle of Paul to the Corinthians the writer unconsciously reveals his own character and lays bare his heart. We see his unquestioning faith, his absolute devotion to Christ, his unselfishness, his prayerfulness, his constant gratitude, his indignation at the enemies of the gospel, his sensitiveness to false charges, his desire for the prayers and his dependence upon the sympathy of friends, his tact, his courtesy, and his love.

Furthermore, some idea is given of the missionary methods of the great apostle. He has sought to establish the church in the great centers of population. Driven out of Philippi, he has begun work in the more important city of Thessalonica. He has not confined his work to preaching in the synagogue, nor has he been discouraged by the opposition of his enemies. He has gathered about him little companies of inquirers, and has gone from house to house dealing with his converts with the courage of a father and the tenderness of a mother.

The character of these converts and the church into which they have been gathered is likewise made clear. We are given at least a glimpse of an early Christian church in all the freshness of its young life. We note its zeal for evangelistic work, its fidelity under persecution, its rapidly developing Christian virtues. It was not free from faults, nor beyond the peril of gross sin. Doctrine was in some points perverted; spiritual leaders were not always obeyed. The exact office of these leaders is not made clear. They were expected to admonish the disorderly and to encourage the faint-hearted, and to them submission was to be given. They evidently presided at the gatherings for praise, instruction, and prayer. The church was notable for its courage, its charity, and its brotherly love.

The peculiar value of these epistles consists, however, in the fact that they are the earliest extant letters of Paul and probably the earliest existing specimens of Christian literature. They, therefore, embody not merely the missionary message of the great apostle, but the content of the original gospel. Their authenticity and approximate date are not seriously questioned. They may have been written as early as A.D. 48, and certainly are not to be placed later than A.D. 53.

Here then are documents which were produced scarcely twenty years after the resurrection of Christ. What then becomes of the absurd claims of those who insist that the Christ of the Gospels and the Christianity of Paul were products of the imagination, and were legends which grew up in the latter part of the first century?

When writing these epistles, Paul already had been preaching more than fourteen years, and Christ's apostles were quite familiar with the gospel which Paul proclaimed. This gospel is set forth in these letters, and therefore is brought again before the men who were the faithful friends and companions of Christ; and the conceptions here given of his person and work are in exact accord with his own self-revelation to his followers.

As one reviews these letters to the Thessalonians it is surprising to note what a wide range of truth is embraced in this primitive gospel as proclaimed by Paul. The letters, as has been stated, are not dogmatic and doctrinal, but personal and practical. Their teaching is mainly ethical. It has to do with industry, with purity, with honest and holy living, with brotherly love and hope and right conduct.

However, all this life and experience and all these virtues are definitely related to faith. Paul never thinks of divorcing morality and religion. He always bases duty upon doctrine, and the exhortations contained in these epistles are all connected with great Christian verities. The doctrinal statements are the more impressive because they are stated incidentally. Their truth is presupposed. Acceptance of them is taken for granted.

These doctrines include the personality and Fatherhood of God. He is the Author of the gospel which Paul proclaims. He has called believers to a new life, and they must walk worthily of him. His Kingdom and glory are the consummation of the highest human hopes.

As to Christ, he is united with the Father in essential equality; to him prayer is offered, and from him the new life issues. His death and resurrection and redeeming work are the fundamental assumption of the believer's faith. His coming in glory is the final goal of the believer's hope.

The Holy Spirit is represented as the Agent who imparts power to the gospel message, and assurance and joy and gifts of service to the members of the church.

The one doctrine, however, particularly emphasized is that of the Second Coming of Christ. Here Paul speaks definitely and clearly but with notable sanity and restraint. What he writes and what he refrains from writing could be understood fully only by one who knew the teaching Paul had given to the Thessalonians previously, and the exact misconceptions of the doctrine which were disturbing the church. The view of the return of Christ taken by Paul avoids both the extreme views of modern thought. There are those today who predict the collapse of civilization and who see the world hastening onward to its ruin. In contrast with these pessimists there are the shallow optimists who believe that everything is for the best, who dream of nothing but progress, who trust that a social revolution is about to bring the world to its age of gold.

In contrast with both is the prophetic outlook of the apostle as set forth in these epistles. He sees evil more clearly than does the darkest pessimist. He finds its essence to be lawlessness. This is to be finally embodied in a "man of sin," who will claim universal sovereignty and demand to be worshiped as divine.

Yet beyond this scene of darkness Paul describes a future brightness, surpassing the dream of the most hopeful optimist. The appearance of the man of sin is to be followed by the appearance of the Son of Man. The destruction of "the lawless one" is to result in the absolute triumph and the unlimited reign of Christ. As to details Paul gives little to satisfy but enough to inspire comfort and cheer. He sets no dates. He warns against feverish excitement. He urges Christians to be ready for their Lord's return, and on that great event he centers the hope of the church and of the world.

THE OUTLINE

I
PERSONAL

I Thess., chs. 1 to 3

A. THE SALUTATION   Ch. 1:1

1 Paul, and Silvanus, and Timothy, unto the church of the Thessalonians in God the Father and the Lord Jesus Christ: Grace to you and peace.

The name Paul is arresting. Standing at the head of this epistle it gives significance to all that the letter contains. Paul occupies a place of supreme importance among the followers of Christ, and his epistles form the most precious group of letters in all the literature of the world. This, the first in the group, was written within two decades after the ascension of Christ, and some fifteen years before the death of the apostle. Paul was on his historic second missionary journey. He was laboring in the city of Corinth. Recently he had been rejoined by his companions, Silvanus and Timothy. The latter had returned from a special mission to Thessalonica, and the report he brought was the occasion of this First Epistle. Silvanus had been chosen by Paul to take the place of Barnabas, the comrade of his previous journey. In the narrative of The Acts he is known as Silas, probably his Roman surname. He appears to have been a man of prominence in the church at Jerusalem. He was mentioned as the associate of Paul in founding the church at Thessalonica, but after the writing of the Thessalonian letters his name never appears in connection with the great apostle. Timothy, apparently a much younger man, who joined Paul at Lystra and assisted him in a subordinate position, rarely left Paul for any considerable portion of time, but became his beloved and constant companion to the end of the apostle's career.

The union of the three names, "Paul, and Silvanus, and Timothy," in the superscription of the epistle has been taken as an indication of a joint authorship. Such an authorship is further indicated by the use of the first person plural, which appears throughout the Thessalonian epistles with a regularity unparalleled in any subsequent writings of Paul. However, there can be no doubt that Paul was "the primary and principal author." In at least three places he reveals himself as the actual composer of the epistle. (Chs. 2:18; 3:5; 5:27.) Nevertheless, his mention of Silvanus and Timothy is not merely a matter of courtesy. He names them with himself as the "joint founders and pastors" of the Thessalonian church; and the use of the first person plural, while at times referring to Paul himself, usually indicates that he is intending to express feelings and sentiments and beliefs in which he unites with his companions, Silvanus and Timothy.

He does not here call himself "an apostle," as is usual in his later letters. His authority was not specially questioned in Thessalonica. Then, also, this letter is too personal and informal to make such a claim necessary or fitting, and it is further possible that he wishes to place his two companions on the same footing with himself.

The very mention of the three names Paul, Silvanus, and Timothy, here introduced as the authors of the letter, illustrates the mixed character of the early church. Paul and Silvanus were both Jews who possessed Roman citizenship and bore Roman surnames. Timothy had a Greek name and a Greek father, but his mother was a Jewess. Thus the Roman and Greek and Jewish elements formed the substance of that civilization in which the Christian church came to birth.

The particular local church to which the epistle is addressed is called "the church of the Thessalonians in God the Father and the Lord Jesus Christ." The word translated "church" meant originally "any public assembly of citizens summoned by a herald." Here the assembly is defined first by the name of the city to which it belongs, and then by the words which denote its spiritual character and distinguish it from the many political and civil and religious associations then existing in the city of Thessalonica. The phrase is freely rendered, "To the assembly of Thessalonians acknowledging God as Father and Jesus Christ as Lord, and gathered together in this twofold name." These terms indicate the true origin and character of the church. They include all that upon which the church rests and for which it exists. It is a company of believers who know themselves to be children of God their Father, who obey and worship Jesus as their Lord and Savior, who are united in this common faith and service, and who share together a new and divinely imparted life.

As was customary in letters of Paul's day, the names of the authors and readers are followed by a greeting: "Grace to you and peace." Here, as commonly stated, the usual Greek form of salutation, somewhat altered, is united with the Hebrew form, translated "peace." However, the word "grace," χάρις, used by Paul resembles the popular Greek salutation "greeting," χαίρειν, in sound rather than in sense. "Grace" has been called the "watchword of Paul." He employs it twice as often as do all the other New Testament writers combined. By it he signifies the sum of all the blessings which God bestows through Christ upon undeserving men. These blessings are received by faith, and the result is "peace." Thus the latter word describes these benefits as enjoyed by believers. It denotes the harmony with God secured by Christ, but also the inner tranquillity of spirit resulting from such conscious harmony. "Grace" points to God as the Source of the highest good. "Peace" refers to man as the recipient of divine favor. Both grace and peace, as gifts of God, become habits and qualities of the human soul.

Therefore, in his salutation, Paul expresses the prayer

that his readers may be granted in increasing measure both "grace . . . and peace." This form of greeting may be regarded as having been coined by Paul. In more or less expanded form it appears in the superscription of each of his epistles. It may be said to summarize his entire gospel. Thus two words, in common use, when touched by the Spirit of Christ, have been transformed into treasure houses of inspired truth.

B. THE THANKSGIVING   Ch. 1:2-10

2 We give thanks to God always for you all, making mention of you in our prayers; 3 remembering without ceasing your work of faith and labor of love and patience of hope in our Lord Jesus Christ, before our God and Father; 4 knowing, brethren beloved of God, your election, 5 how that our gospel came not unto you in word only, but also in power, and in the Holy Spirit, and in much assurance; even as ye know what manner of men we showed ourselves toward you for your sake. 6 And ye became imitators of us, and of the Lord, having received the word in much affliction, with joy of the Holy Spirit; 7 so that ye became an ensample to all that believe in Macedonia and in Achaia. 8 For from you hath sounded forth the word of the Lord, not only in Macedonia and Achaia, but in every place your faith to God-ward is gone forth; so that we need not to speak anything. 9 For they themselves report concerning us what manner of entering in we had unto you; and how ye turned unto God from idols, to serve a living and true God, 10 and to wait for his Son from heaven, whom he raised from the dead, even Jesus, who delivereth us from the wrath to come.

The salutation or inscription of the epistle contains the names of the writers, a designation of the persons addressed, and a greeting. In further conformity to letters of the same period, the epistle begins with an expression of gratitude and good wishes. Such an opening thanksgiving is found in practically all of Paul's epistles, a notable ex-

ception being the Epistle to the Galatians.   Here the
thanksgiving consists of what is in reality one long and ir-
regular sentence comprising the remainder of the first
chapter.   This thanksgiving is not merely conventional
and complimentary.   It is sincerely affectionate and aims
not only to express gratefulness, but to awaken in the readers new trust in God and to stimulate them to wider efforts for Christ.

The immediate ground of the thanksgiving is the memory of the Christian virtues manifested by the readers.
The ultimate ground is the knowledge of their divine
election.   This election is proved by the manner in which
the gospel has been preached among them, by the way in
which it has been received by them, and, further, by the
widespread report of the new faith and life of the converts.

"We give thanks to God always for you all, making
mention of you in our prayers."   Thus the writers affirm
that whenever they pray they remember their friends at
Thessalonica, and as they remember them their first feeling is that of gratitude to God.   The warmth of this gratitude is shown by its being constant and inclusive.   "Always for you all," are the words.

The remembrance which causes this gratitude is that of
the "faith" and "love" and "hope" of the readers.   Thus,
for the first time in the writings of Paul, this famous triad
of Christian virtues is mentioned.   The order is natural, as
"faith" rests on the past, "love" acts in the present, "hope"
looks to the future.

These virtues, however, are regarded here not so much
for what they are in themselves as for what they secure.
It is the "work of faith and labor of love and patience of
hope" which are remembered.   The "work of faith" is the
work which faith accomplishes; the "labor of love" is
the effort which love prompts; the "patience of hope" is the
endurance which hope inspires.   The first is the work
which faith accomplishes in one's own life; the second is
the labor undertaken for others; the third is the patience

of those whose hope centers upon Christ.

Thus the "work of faith" does not have its modern popular meaning of a religious, philanthropic, or evangelistic enterprise, undertaken in exclusive dependence upon God. It refers to the entire effort of faith upon the life and experience and character of the individual believer.

"Labor" translates a word which implies effort, toil, and activity carried to the limit of endurance. The "labor of love," therefore, denotes the toilsome effort which love is willing to exert in the service of others.

"Patience" is not mere passive endurance. It is heroic perseverance and manly constancy. In this passage it is mentioned as a virtue supported by "hope." The latter denotes a confident expectation of future good. Here hope is described as fixed upon Christ, whose personal appearing is the great reality to which the writers of this epistle continually revert.

This hope is defined not only by the words, "In our Lord Jesus Christ," but also by the phrase, "Before our God and Father." Some readers prefer to unite the latter phrase with the word "remembering." Thus it is in the presence of God that hope is operating, or it is in the divine presence that Paul and his companions bear in grateful remembrance the virtues of their Thessalonian friends.

The further source of their gratitude, the deeper ground of their thanksgiving, is the confident assurance that the readers are the objects of a divine election: "Knowing, brethren beloved of God, your election." That the members of the Christian brotherhood have been thus chosen and called of God, Paul is absolutely certain. As to the mystery involved, or the divine mode of operation, he here has nothing to say further than his intimating that the election is due to the abiding, determinate love of God.

The certainty of this election to membership in the family of God is based upon the effectiveness of Paul's ministry and upon the genuine character of the Thessalonians' faith. Paul cannot doubt that God's purpose was being worked out when God's presence and power were so manifest. The Holy Spirit unquestionably was in those who preached and in those who welcomed the word.

"Our gospel came not unto you in word only, but also in power, and in the Holy Spirit, and in much assurance." This gospel which Paul and his comrades preached is elsewhere called "the gospel of God," or "the gospel of Christ." It denotes the good news of salvation provided through the divine person and redeeming work of Christ. When proclaimed in Thessalonica it had proved to be no mere matter of words or of human reasoning. It was attended by transforming "power." It came with an ardor which only the Holy Spirit could have inspired and with a personal conviction and an unfaltering confidence on the part of the messengers. The hearers could testify "what manner of men" the apostle and his friends had shown themselves to be, how full of the Holy Spirit, how evidently sent of God to secure his purpose and to accomplish his work of grace and of love.

The divine "election" of the Thessalonians was proved by the preaching they had heard. Even more forcibly was it demonstrated by the conduct of the converts: "Ye became imitators of us, and of the Lord." It is rather startling to have the writers mention themselves first, before "the Lord," as the examples that were followed by the readers. It might seem to denote self-consciousness or pride. Rather, in humility the words, "And of the Lord," are added to show the real Source of what the Thessalonians imitated. They followed the messengers as the messengers followed Christ. Then, too, only one particular is here specified. It was that they "received the word in much affliction, with joy of the Holy Spirit." They welcomed the gospel message with joy, even amid bitter persecution. This union of joy with suffering was illustrated indeed in the life of Paul, and more impressively still in the life of the Master. Joy as an accompaniment of pain is not natural. It is attributed to divine power. Its source is the indwelling Holy Spirit. That the Thessalonians, while afflicted and distressed, had entered joyfully upon their new manner of life was a decisive proof of their "election." Such conduct could be attributed only to the power of God.

Further evidence of this "election" is found in the fact that the imitation of Christ and his witnesses on the part of the Thessalonians made them models for imitation by wide circles of believers: "So that ye became an ensample to all that believe in Macedonia and in Achaia." The two provinces mentioned comprised at that time the whole of Greece. The Christians of the entire country, therefore, had been inspired by the example of the Thessalonians.

This statement was none too strong, as is shown by the verses which follow (vs. 8-10). The fact is that from this church as a center the gospel message had sounded out as a clear trumpet blast, not only in the places mentioned, but everywhere that the faith of the Thessalonians toward God had been reported. In addition to this common report the writers "need not to speak anything." All those from whom such a report has come are ready to testify as to the nature and success of the apostle's work in Thessalonica—"What manner of entering in we had unto you"— and also to bear witness to the effect of this testimony upon the readers.

"Ye turned unto God from idols, to serve a living and true God," writes Paul, "and to wait for his Son from heaven." These words form an admirable description of true conversion. Men naturally worship "idols," mere "phantoms without substance," false, lifeless gods. Those who heed the gospel call forsake such deities to serve the one "living and true God"—"true" not only in contrast with false, but as fulfilling the whole conception and ideal of deity. To such a God, believers turn with the devotion of loving servants, dedicated to doing his will. Then, too, the converts turn their faces upward in confident hope. They "wait for his Son from heaven." This expectation of a returning Lord was an essential element in Paul's first preaching at Thessalonica. It is an ever-recurring theme in these epistles. It was an essential element in the faith of the early church.

This Son of God, who is to reappear, is further described by the words, "Whom he raised from the dead, even Jesus, who delivereth us from the wrath to come." The resurrection and ascension were the proof of the divine Sonship of Jesus, the prelude to his return. A crucified, risen, coming Christ is the Object of a believer's faith and love and hope. He already has given deliverance from the guilt and power of sin. He will deliver from the coming wrath of God. This wrath is not to be conceived as angry resentment but as the divine displeasure with sin which is inseparable from the holiness and love of God. From all the future consequences of sin, from all dread of a judgment to come, Christ sets the believer free. His return will complete the salvation already begun. His glorious appearing is the inspiring, purifying hope of all those who put their trust in him.

C. PAUL'S MINISTRY AMONG THE THESSALONIANS   Ch. 2:1-12

1 For yourselves, brethren, know our entering in unto you, that it hath not been found vain: 2 but having suffered before and been shamefully treated, as ye know, at Philippi, we waxed bold in our God to speak unto you the gospel of God in much conflict. 3 For our exhortation is not of error, nor of uncleanness, nor in guile: 4 but even as we have been approved of God to be intrusted with the gospel, so we speak; not as pleasing men, but God who proveth our hearts. 5 For neither at any time were we found using words of flattery, as ye know, nor a cloak of covetousness, God is witness; 6 nor seeking glory of men, neither from you nor from others, when we might have claimed authority as apostles of Christ. 7 But we were gentle in the midst of you, as when a nurse cherisheth her

*own children: 8 even so, being affectionately desirous of
you, we were well pleased to impart unto you, not the gospel of God only, but also our own souls, because ye were
become very dear to us.   9 For ye remember, brethren, our
labor and travail: working night and day, that we might not
burden any of you, we preached unto you the gospel of
God.   10 Ye are witnesses, and God also, how holily and
righteously and unblamably we behaved ourselves toward
you that believe: 11 as ye know how we dealt with each
one of you, as a father with his own children, exhorting
you, and encouraging you, and testifying, 12 to the end
that ye should walk worthily of God, who calleth you into
his own kingdom and glory.*

The first chapter of the epistle is in substance a thanksgiving based on the knowledge of the divine election of the
Thessalonians.   This election is proved by the character of
the apostle's mission and by the conduct of the believers.
Paul now enlarges upon the nature of this mission (vs.
1-12) and then upon the reception the Thessalonians had
given to the gospel message (vs. 13-16).

The purpose of Paul in dwelling more fully upon his
ministry in Thessalonica is evidently to meet the criticisms
and accusations of his enemies, as reported to him by Timothy.   The passage contains an admirable message for the
guidance of ministers and missionaries and Christian workers in modern times.   It might be regarded as a manual
for pastors.   However, as Paul reveals his own motives
and aims, as he lays bare his very heart, one feels that
the impulses and purposes disclosed are those which should
animate not only public servants but every follower of
Christ.

Reference has already been made to the common report,
widely disseminated, as to the character of Paul's ministry
at Thessalonica.   There is, however, no need thus to repeat
the witness of others.   The Thessalonians themselves can
testify to the effective nature of Paul's service among them:
"For yourselves, brethren, know our entering in unto you,

that it hath not been found vain," empty, void of reality
and power. It was a divine mission, as manifested, first
of all, in the courage of the apostle: "Having suffered before and been shamefully treated, as ye know, at Philippi,
we waxed bold in our God to speak unto you the gospel of
God in much conflict." It is to be noted that the courage
of the apostle, and the other virtues which he proceeds to
mention, are all traced to a divine Source. His claims are
no idle boasting. His defense is no exhibition of vanity
and pride. He does mention his courage, but it is in the
words, "We waxed bold in our God." Such courage was
worthy of mention. Beaten and imprisoned, "shamefully
treated" and insulted at Philippi, the apostle had come directly to Thessalonica and there, in the midst of much opposition—"in much conflict"—he had proclaimed the gospel for which they had endured such contumely, suffering,
and shame. Surely such boldness was proof of a divine
mission and of the sustaining grace of God.

In further defense, and in contrast with many wander-
ing religious impostors of his day, Paul sets forth the sincerity and purity of his motives and the motives of his fellow missionaries: "For our exhortation is not of error"—
our appeal is not rooted in false beliefs; it is not "of uncleanness," or connected with licentious practices, as is
the teaching of many false cults; it is not "in guile," craftily
designed to deceive the hearers.

On the contrary, as those who "have been approved of
God" and have been "intrusted with the gospel," so they
speak—concerned not with "pleasing men, but God," who
tests the heart.

This which was true of the motives of the apostles was
also true of their conduct, which the readers could recall.
Never at any time were they "found using words of flattery" to secure some selfish end, "nor a cloak of covetousness," an outward pretext designed to conceal a secret
greed for gain. God himself could testify to their sincerity
and unselfishness. They had been so far from seeking

"glory of men," either of the Thessalonians or of others, that they had refrained from demanding support and honor, and had not "claimed [the] authority" which was due them "as apostles of Christ."

In addition to the boldness of their preaching and the purity of their motives, Paul mentions the tenderness shown by himself and his fellow workers: "We were gentle in the midst of you, as when a nurse cherisheth her own children." One does not always think of Paul as a man of emotion, of tenderness, and of tears. He is often pictured as intellectual, but cold and keen and unfeeling. In reality he was a man of sympathy, of a tender heart, of self-sacrificing love. "Even so," he writes, "being affectionately desirous of you, we were well pleased to impart unto you, not the gospel of God only, but also our own souls, because ye were become very dear to us."

This loving devotion to his converts the Thessalonian Christians themselves could attest. Paul had a right to be supported by those to whom he had brought the gospel and to whom he ministered in things spiritual. The Thessalonians, however, could recall that he had not claimed this right, but had labored at tentmaking so that he might not be a burden to the church: "For ye remember, brethren, our labor and travail: working night and day, that we might not burden any of you, we preached unto you the gospel of God."

Not only were the motives of Paul and his fellow workers holy and unselfish, but their lives had been pure and consistent. To this not only the readers but God himself could testify: "Ye are witnesses, and God also, how holily and righteously and unblamably we behaved ourselves toward you that believe."

In his personal dealings with his converts, Paul had shown not only the tenderness of a nurse but the wisdom of a father. He had exhorted and encouraged them to daily lives worthy of the God who had called them into his eternal fellowship: "Ye know how we dealt with each one of you, as a father with his own children, exhorting you, and encouraging you, and testifying, to the end that ye should walk worthily of God, who calleth you into his own kingdom and glory."

In reading such a passage, in which Paul is evidently defending himself against the attacks of his enemies, it is rather distressing to note that even such a man could not escape the slander and false charges which emanate from suspicion and malice and envy. On the other hand, such a picture of a Christian pastor, drawn with such conscious sincerity and honesty, warns all the followers of Christ against the temptation of avarice and ambition and inspires them to emulate the courage, the purity, the tenderness, the self-sacrifice, and the fidelity which the apostle claimed and which all who knew him could testify he had embodied in his life.

D. PAUL'S RECEPTION BY THE THESSALONIANS   Ch. 2:13-16

13 And for this cause we also thank God without ceasing, that, when ye received from us the word of the message, even the word of God, ye accepted it not as the word of men, but, as it is in truth, the word of God, which also worketh in you that believe. 14 For ye, brethren, became imitators of the churches of God which are in Judæa in Christ Jesus: for ye also suffered the same things of your own countrymen, even as they did of the Jews; 15 who both killed the Lord Jesus and the prophets, and drove out us, and please not God, and are contrary to all men; 16 forbidding us to speak to the Gentiles that they may be saved; to fill up their sins always: but the wrath is come upon them to the uttermost.

In the opening chapter of his epistle, Paul has declared that the divine "election" of the Thessalonian Christians has been attested by his ministry among them and by their reception of his message. In the beginning of the second

chapter he has enlarged upon the first of these proofs, setting forth the courage and self-devotion of his ministry.
He now turns to speak more fully of the reception afforded
to his ministry in Thessalonica.   However, there is in this
second chapter, in both these paragraphs, a new emphasis.
Paul is not only establishing the divine "election" of his
readers.   He is evidently answering false charges made by
his enemies.

However, as the "election" of the Thessalonians is the
ground of the thanksgiving with which the epistle opens,
so here that which has been a proof of the election is given
again as a reason for praise.   "For this cause we also thank
God without ceasing," writes the apostle, "that, when ye
received from us the word of the message, even the word
of God, ye accepted it not as the word of men, but, as it is
in truth, the word of God, which also worketh in you that
believe."   The phrase, "For this cause," throws the
thought back to the preceding paragraph.   The toil and
self-sacrifice of the apostles made them the more ready to
thank God for the reception given to their message and
for the patient endurance of the Thessalonians.   They had
received this message "not as the word of men, but, as it is
in truth, the word of God."   Paul thus expresses his view
of the gospel.   It is no human invention, no result of the
apostle's own reasoning and experience.   It is absolutely
divine in its origin.   Its reception results in the manifestation of a divine transforming power, "which also worketh
in you that believe."   The effect of the gospel is condi-
tioned upon faith.   When the gospel message is welcomed
as the very word of God it never fails to produce such
Christian graces as love and joy and peace and patience.

It is the last of these virtues which Paul has particularly
in mind.   The patient endurance of persecution was a
proof that the gospel was working in the lives of the Thessalonians: "Ye, brethren, became imitators of the churches
of God which are in Judæa in Christ Jesus: for ye also suffered the same things of your own countrymen, even as

they did of the Jews." The imitation consisted not only
in suffering, but in suffering with patience and courage. It
was like the imitation described in the previous chapter,
where the same readers were reminded of how they had
"received the word in much affliction, with joy of the Holy
Spirit."

How bitter had been the affliction endured by the Ju-
dean churches none knew so well as Paul himself. He
had been the leading persecutor of these very churches.
He had resorted to imprisonment and scourging and ago-
nizing death to make these Christians recant. What the
Thessalonians had suffered we do not know. Their anguish must have been great to warrant such a comparison.
Great, too, must have been the grace of God which enabled them to bear such torture with patient fortitude. In
the first chapter this patience is used as a proof of divine
election. Here it is a proof of the power of the gospel
which the Thessalonians had received.

The mention of the Jews as persecutors led Paul to make
a brief but bitter indictment of his fellow countrymen, unparalleled in severity by any other reference to them in all
his writings. He declares that they "killed the Lord Jesus." This was the supreme sin of the nation. Yet it was
in accordance with their uniform treatment of the messengers of God. They also had "killed . . . the prophets,"
before the coming of Christ; they "drove out" the apostles
who followed him. In their opposition to the work of the
Christian missionaries, in their persecution of the Thessalonian believers, and in the endeavor to discredit Paul and
his companions, they were opposing the will of God and
depriving men of their highest good. As the indictment
declares, "[They] please not God, and are contrary to all
men; forbidding us to speak to the Gentiles that they may
be saved." In so doing they were filling to its brim their
cup of iniquity. Their violent and rancorous rejection of
the gospel was being brought to its climax by their jealous
and cruel determination that this gospel should not be

preached to the Gentiles. In every step taken they were acting in accordance with the stubborn unbelief shown by their fathers. They were proceeding "to fill up their sins always."

However, if the cup of guilt was overflowing, so was the cup of judgment: "The wrath is come upon them to the uttermost." The exact form in which this divine wrath had appeared or was about to be manifested is not stated. The reference could hardly point definitely to the destruction of Jerusalem. That tragedy did not occur until about twenty years later. Nor do we know of any other event which the writers may have had in mind. The expression is probably general, not specific. The spiritual blindness of the nation and the very depth of its depravity showed that its day of grace must have ended and the hour had struck in which the vials of divine wrath would be outpoured.

It must not be supposed, however, that Paul had lost his love for Israel, nor his hope for his own race, the Jews. A few years later he penned his prediction of a great national conversion. Israel would be saved and the salvation of Israel would result in blessing to the whole world.

E. THE MISSION OF TIMOTHY
Chs. 2:17 to 3:5

17 But we, brethren, being bereaved of you for a short season, in presence not in heart, endeavored the more exceedingly to see your face with great desire: 18 because we would fain have come unto you, I Paul once and again; and Satan hindered us. 19 For what is our hope, or joy, or crown of glorying? Are not even ye, before our Lord Jesus at his coming? 20 For ye are our glory and our joy.

1 Wherefore when we could no longer forbear, we thought it good to be left behind at Athens alone; 2 and sent Timothy, our brother and God's minister in the gospel of Christ, to establish you, and to comfort you concerning your faith; 3 that no man be moved by these afflictions; for yourselves know that hereunto we are appointed. 4

For verily, when we were with you, we told you beforehand
that we are to suffer affliction; even as it came to pass, and
ye know. 5 For this cause I also, when I could no longer
forbear, sent that I might know your faith, lest by any
means the tempter had tempted you, and our labor should
be in vain.

Christian friendships are of priceless value. Such is the
main message of these paragraphs. Here Paul pours out
his very heart in expressing his love for the Thessalonians.
He explains that his devotion to them made him willing
to be left alone in Athens and to send to them his beloved
associate, Timothy, that he might learn of their condition
and might strengthen their faith.

Various reasons are assigned for such a vehement expression of affection. Paul has been maligned by his enemies. They have misrepresented the character of his ministry in Thessalonica and seem to have insinuated that his
failure to return was due to a lack of interest in his converts. The first charge he has met by reviewing his work
in Thessalonica, and by describing the reception it had received. (Ch. 2:1-16.) This was Paul's defense of his
conduct. It was his *"apologia pro vita sua."* He is now
explaining his absence. (Chs. 2:17 to 3:5.) It is called
his *"apologia pro absentia sua."*

However, the passionate language, more probably is
due, not to any reported criticism of the apostle's failure
to return to Thessalonica, but rather to the loving sympathy felt for his friends and to his deep solicitude for their
welfare.

Paul had been compelled to flee to Berea. From thence
he had gone to Athens. Yet he had sought continually for
an opportunity to return to the Thessalonians. Only
when this was found impossible had he sent Timothy back
to act in his own stead, to strengthen their faith, and to report their state.

"But we, brethren," writes the apostle, possibly contrast-

ing his love with the malice of Jews of whom he had just
written, "being bereaved of you for a short season"—as
orphaned children, broken-hearted and alone—"in presence not in heart"—that is, out of sight but not out of
mind—"endeavored the more exceedingly to see your face
with great desire." A real effort had been made. The determination was fixed not only once, but "once and again."
"Satan hindered us," Paul declares. What obstacles the
adversary had placed in the path one can only conjecture.

It is unwise to interpret events too narrowly, but the inspired writers usually point to a personal embodiment of
evil as the ultimate source of those forces and conditions
which tend to thwart the cause of Christ and to occasion
his followers disappointment and distress.

Paul's failure to revisit Thessalonica was due to no lack
of love on his part. "For what is our hope, or joy, or
crown of glorying?" asks Paul; and he at once adds, "Are
not even ye?" These dear friends are the objects of his
highest hopes, the source of his deepest joy, and of them
he is more proud than a champion is of his chaplet or a
monarch of his crown. These relations to his converts will
be complete "before our Lord Jesus at his coming." In
the writings of Paul, there is frequent mention of that glorious event which was so constantly in his mind and is so
prominent in these letters to the Thessalonians. At the
appearing of Christ, Paul's hopes for his followers will be
realized, his joy because of them will be full, his pride in
them will be justified. "For ye are," he adds, "[and ye
will be] our glory and our joy."

Such deep affection for his friends made separation from
them, and ignorance of their welfare, intolerable. "Wherefore when we could no longer forbear," he writes, "we
thought it good to be left behind at Athens alone; and sent
Timothy, our brother and God's minister in the gospel of
Christ." The words "left behind" and "alone" intimate
that the mission of Timothy involved a real sacrifice on the
part of Paul. It was a sacrifice of love. The description

of the messenger as "our brother" and "God's minister in the gospel of Christ" reveals Paul's loving appreciation of the worth of his young companion and the deep significance of his work. The purpose of Timothy's mission is summed up in the words, "To establish you, and to comfort you concerning your faith." That there was need of such strengthening and cheer Paul and his readers knew full well. The bitter hatred which had driven Paul from the city had been expressed in persecuting the Christians whom he had left behind. Timothy, therefore, had been sent back on this mission of encouragement to prevent any persons from being allured from the right path in the midst of their sufferings; or, as the apostle states, "That no man be moved by these afflictions."

Their sufferings should have occasioned no surprise. They were fully aware that suffering for the sake of Christ is a necessary experience in Christian life: "For yourselves know that hereunto we are appointed." As to this the apostle had warned them: "For verily, when we were with you, we told you beforehand that we are to suffer affliction." That this prediction had been fulfilled they were only too well aware: "Even as it came to pass, and ye know."

"For this cause," expecting such continued and increasing persecution of the Thessalonian Christians, Paul, as well as Silas—but Paul, as the one most keenly alive to the peril of his converts—had sent to learn whether their faith was steadfast, or, "That I might know your faith." He feared "lest by any means the tempter had tempted" them. The sufferings are attributed to Satan as their source. He might have taken advantage of their distress to beguile these believers from their faith. If so, the missionary efforts of Paul and his companions in Thessalonica would have been rendered fruitless: "Our labor should be in vain."

This brief but moving recital of the mission of Timothy reveals the throbbing heart of the apostle and indicates how even so mighty a mind was dependent upon the sympathy and assistance of his friends.

F. THE JOYFUL TIDINGS Ch. 3:6-10

6 But when Timothy came even now unto us from you, and brought us glad tidings of your faith and love, and that ye have good remembrance of us always, longing to see us, even as we also to see you; 7 for this cause, brethren, we were comforted over you in all our distress and affliction through your faith: 8 for now we live, if ye stand fast in the Lord. 9 For what thanksgiving can we render again unto God for you, for all the joy wherewith we joy for your sakes before our God; 10 night and day praying exceedingly that we may see your face, and may perfect that which is lacking in your faith?

The anxiety felt by Paul for the Thessalonians had been keen. His fears had been real. After all, men are mortal. It would not have been surprising if, in the anguish of torture and outrage, some had renounced their faith in Christ. What an unspeakable relief, then, had come to Paul when he learned from Timothy that his fears had been unfounded and that amidst all their persecution his converts had stood steadfast in their faith! Nor was it of their faith alone that Timothy had spoken. He had told of their affection for the apostle. He "brought us glad tidings of your faith and love." They cherished his memory; as Timothy reported, "Ye have good remembrance of us always." They were eager for a reunion, as was Paul: "Longing to see us, even as we also to see you."

Such glad tidings dispelled Paul's fears for the Thessalonians. The good news gave the apostle courage to face his own persecution and sufferings. Of such courage there was great need. He had reached Corinth alone without friends or funds. Around him had been a black night of pagan corruption. Against him had been launched the most vicious attacks by the Jews. He had been, at least

figuratively, in the shadow of death. However, the good
news brought by Timothy gave him new life. It was one
of the chief of those factors which brought him in triumph
through what has been called his "Corinthian crisis."

Thus, in view of the steadfast faith and endurance of
the Thessalonians, Paul can write, "For this cause, brethren, we were comforted over you in all our distress and affliction through your faith: for now we live, if ye stand fast
in the Lord." This report of their faith has given him not
only new life but unbounded joy. Words fail him to express his gratitude to God for this gladness which fills his
heart: "For what thanksgiving can we render again unto
God for you, for all the joy wherewith we joy for your
sakes before our God?"

It is to be noted that this rejoicing is said to be "before
our God." Thus, while Paul is thankful for the courage
and faith of his converts, and thus for the success of his
work in Thessalonica, yet it is to God himself that his
thanksgiving is directed—to "our God," "the God and Father of our Lord Jesus Christ."

Furthermore, this joy and gratitude are expressed in
ceaseless prayer that Paul may be permitted to revisit his
friends in Thessalonica and may do something to add to
the completeness of their Christian life, or, in his own
words, "Night and day praying exceedingly that we may
see your face, and may perfect that which is lacking in
your faith." Paul does not impute perfection to his readers. He indicates, however, that their defects are not serious. In the closing sections of the epistle he will give
them instruction and advice, such indeed as he would
bring them were he privileged to see them face to face.
Yet so firm and unshaken has been their faith, so real their
loyalty to him and their allegiance to Christ, that now the
loving heart of the great apostle is filled with joy and gratitude at the report of their condition brought to him by
Timothy, his devoted and trusted friend.

G. PAUL'S PRAYER   Ch. 3:11-13

11 Now may our God and Father himself, and our Lord Jesus, direct our way unto you: 12 and the Lord make you to increase and abound in love one toward another, and toward all men, even as we also do toward you; 13 to the end he may establish your hearts unblamable in holiness before our God and Father, at the coming of our Lord Jesus with all his saints.

It was the custom of Paul to open his epistles with a salutation, a thanksgiving, and a prayer. In this, the first of his letters which has been preserved, he adopts that general course. However, the prayer is long delayed. The thanksgiving which follows the salutation expands into a long series of paragraphs which set forth his ministry to Thessalonica and its reception on the part of his readers. To all these experiences he refers with expressions of gratitude. He then concludes the personal portion of the epistle with a prayer that he may be privileged to revisit his Thessalonian friends and that they, by the power of love, may be prepared for the coming of Christ. The prayer is inseparable from the paragraphs which precede. Its first petition only repeats a request which Paul declares he has been offering continually. As he has just said, "Night and day praying exceedingly that we may see your face," so he continues, "Now may our God and Father himself, and our Lord Jesus, direct our way unto you." After all, the disposition of such matters is in the hands of God. With him is left the question whether or not Paul is to return to Thessalonica. Rather, from him he asks that such a desired visit may be made possible. With the name of God the Father, Paul unites that of "our Lord Jesus" in an implied relationship of equality. It is a clear indication of the view of the person of Christ held by Paul even in the days of his earliest epistles.

The second petition is not for Paul but for his readers. He has just said that he hopes that he may again see their faces and that his coming again may result in supplying any deficiencies in their Christian life. So in this prayer he definitely asks that their love may be made to abound, so that their holiness may be made more complete.

The love for which Paul prays is not only "love one toward another," as a group of Christians, but also "toward all men." The measure or example of such love is found in Paul's own experience: "Even as we also do toward you." The source of love is traced to the Lord Jesus Christ. He is asked by Paul to make the Thessalonians "to increase and abound in love." The result of such love is to be "holiness." This relation of love to other virtues is significant. One might in some sense be holy without being loving. One who loves cannot fail to be holy, for love is the fulfilling of all the law. It seeks the highest welfare of others. Its pure fires burn out all the dross of selfishness and impurity. Thus Paul prays that the love of the Thessalonians may be growing and glowing in order that their "hearts," their inward purposes and desires, may be established. The result then will be that their hearts, their characters, will appear faultlessly holy, or "unblamable in holiness," before God. "Holiness" denotes, first of all, a state of separation from evil and consecration to God, and then such a state of moral purity as naturally results. God alone is the ultimate Judge. He at last will test the hearts to see whether they are free from blame in the sphere of holiness.

Such a final testing and divine approval is associated with the return of Christ. It is to be "at the coming of our Lord Jesus with all his saints." That risen and glorified believers will be in the company of Christ as he appears in majesty and triumph is definitely taught in the following chapter. Indeed, the three paragraphs of that chapter are summed up in the three great words of this prayer: "holiness," discussed in ch. 4:1-8, "love," in vs. 9-12, and the "coming" of our Lord, in vs. 13-18.

II
PRACTICAL

Chs. 4; 5

A. WARNING AGAINST IMPURITY   Ch. 4:1-8

1 Finally then, brethren, we beseech and exhort you in the Lord Jesus, that, as ye received of us how ye ought to walk and to please God, even as ye do walk,—that ye abound more and more. 2 For ye know what charge we gave you through the Lord Jesus. 3 For this is the will of God, even your sanctification, that ye abstain from fornication; 4 that each one of you know how to possess himself of his own vessel in sanctification and honor, 5 not in the passion of lust, even as the Gentiles who know not God; 6 that no man transgress, and wrong his brother in the matter: because the Lord is an avenger in all these things, as also we forewarned you and testified. 7 For God called us not for uncleanness, but in sanctification. 8 Therefore he that rejecteth, rejecteth not man, but God, who giveth his Holy Spirit unto you.

Christianity is eminently practical. Its adherents believe that "truth is in order to goodness" and that there is an inseparable connection between creed and character, between doctrine and duty, between faith and life. Thus Paul's Epistles usually contain sections of doctrine followed by practical sections in which the doctrine is made the basis for exhortation.

In the First Epistle to the Thessalonians the opening chapters are personal. Paul defends himself against the insinuations of his enemies and expresses his affection and love for his converts. The last two chapters are described properly as "practical," and consist of warnings and exhortations.

The opening paragraph consists of a general encouragement to progress in the Christian life and a specific warning against impurity. The introductory word "finally" is
of interest. It introduces the last section of the epistle, and
indicates a transition to other subjects with which the remainder of the letter will be concerned. It does not mean
that the end of the epistle has been reached. Indeed, from
some points of view the most important part of the letter
now begins. A salutation, a thanksgiving, and a prayer
have been written. Here the writer enters upon his practical instruction.

"We beseech and exhort you in the Lord," that is, the
Thessalonians are being addressed as Christians, in view of
their close relation to Christ. They are exhorted "to walk"
as Paul has taught them. "To walk" refers to one's conduct of life. It is a Hebrew expression, used also in describing Enoch: "Enoch walked with God." So these
Christians had been instructed how to walk so as "to please
God." Indeed, they had begun to live in that way: "Even
as ye do walk," writes the apostle. However, he would
have them make progress in their Christian living. He
wants them to do better and better. "That ye abound
more and more" is his exhortation. They are not urged
to begin a Christian life, but to advance on the way that
they have entered. Paul is to give them no new rules or
standards of life. They remember perfectly well the commands he gave when he was with them, commands given
on the authority of Christ: "For ye know what charge we
gave you through the Lord Jesus."

In a single word, the right walk for a Christian, the way
to please God, is purity of life, a holiness resulting from
separation from sin and devotion to the service of God:
"For this is the will of God, even your sanctification."

The apostle proceeds to deal with only one negative aspect of this holy life which is expected of believers. "That
ye abstain from fornication" is the specific demand. The
impurity here forbidden was the cardinal sin of the ancient

world. Even Christians found it difficult to escape from
its taint. There is much to make one believe that in modern life it is among the common and powerful forms of
temptation.

To guard against this peril it is the will of God that
Christians, avoiding prevalent practices, should enter into
the marriage relation and preserve it pure from base passion. Such is the evident purport of Paul's instruction.
There are, however, differing views as to the exact meaning of certain words which he uses, particularly the word
"vessel." Does he refer to one's body or to one's wife
when he says, "That each one of you know how to possess
himself of his own vessel in sanctification and honor"?
Quite probably the apostle has in mind the holy and rev-
erent regard which a husband should have toward a wife,
in contrast with the low and degrading views of marriage
so prevalent among the Gentiles, with their imperfect
knowledge of God.

Such pure and honorable marriage should prevent one
from invading the sanctity of another's home: "That no
man transgress, and wrong his brother in the matter."
There are added solemn sanctions which should make one
obedient to these divine requirements as to personal purity.

First of all is the fact concerning which Paul had given
solemn warning—that "the Lord is an avenger in all these
things." There is no form of sin so certain to be followed
by pain and by penalty, in time or in eternity, as impurity.
From this punishment there is no possible escape.

In the second place, impurity is directly opposed to the
purpose of God in calling us into the Christian life: "For
God called us not for uncleanness, but in sanctification."
Furthermore, God has given "his Holy Spirit" to be an
abiding Presence with the believer, the Spirit whose very
purpose is to sanctify and to produce holiness of life.
Therefore, to be guilty of impurity is to defy God and to
insult the Giver of the highest and best Gift, for "he that
rejecteth, rejecteth not man, but God."

These words were written from Corinth, a city notorious for vice. They are strikingly similar to words subsequently written by Paul to Christians in Corinth, referring to the same prevalent sin: "Know ye not that your body is a temple of the Holy Spirit which is in you, which ye have from God? . . . glorify God therefore in your body."

B. EXHORTATION TO LOVE AND INDUSTRY
Ch. 4:9-12

9 But concerning love of the brethren ye have no need that one write unto you: for ye yourselves are taught of God to love one another; 10 for indeed ye do it toward all the brethren that are in all Macedonia. But we exhort you, brethren, that ye abound more and more; 11 and that ye study to be quiet, and to do your own business, and to work with your hands, even as we charged you; 12 that ye may walk becomingly toward them that are without, and may have need of nothing.

The readers have been exhorted, first of all, to purity. They now are exhorted to love. Having been warned against the cardinal vice of the heathen world, they are urged to increase in the fundamental virtue of the Christian life. This virtue is to be shown in a life of peaceful industry.

On this subject of love, however, it is hardly necessary for the apostle to speak: "Concerning love of the brethren ye have no need that one write unto you." It is almost unnecessary for two reasons. First, "ye yourselves are taught of God." This not only means that they have received divine instruction or a divine command but also intimates that, as those who have been born of God and have his Spirit in their hearts, they have learned the great lesson of unfailing love.

In the second place, they need little in the way of exhortation because they already are doing what they have been divinely taught: "For indeed ye do it toward all the

brethren that are in all Macedonia." All their fellow believers throughout the whole province in which they live
have been the objects of their affectionate regard or re-
cipients of their loving help.

While this is all true, yet love is something which can
grow and can be manifested ever more widely. Therefore,
Paul adds, "But we exhort you, brethren, that ye abound
more and more" in this essential grace. Furthermore, a
situation had arisen in the church which required a special
exercise of brotherly love. Certain members of the church,
possibly influenced by their expectation of a speedy return
of Christ, were restless, meddlesome, and idle, neglecting
their daily tasks and depending upon others to supply
their needs. The situation seems to have been so serious
that the advice of the apostles had been asked. They do
not forbid the exercise of charity. They encourage it.
However, they do urge upon all believers to "study to be
quiet," that is, to make an earnest endeavor to be calm
and collected and tranquil of spirit. Faith in Christ and
the promise of his return give no excuse for excitement, for
fanaticism, for unrest. A Christian should seek to maintain a quiet mind and to preserve peace with his fellow
believers.

He should also avoid intruding upon the affairs of others, or imposing on them his peculiar beliefs. He should
not be meddlesome. "Study"—or, "Make an earnest endeavor"—writes the apostle, ". . . to do your own business"; or, in modern homely parlance, "to attend to your
own affairs," "to mind your own business."

One must not be guilty of idleness. No religious theories, no study of prophecy can excuse one for neglecting
his daily task. Manual labor is honorable and dignified.
Paul had so taught the Thessalonians when he was with
them. "Work with your hands," he writes, "even as we
charged you."

Two reasons are assigned for seeking "to be quiet" and
for avoiding meddlesomeness and idleness. The first is

that believers may not bring Christianity into disrepute with unbelievers; and the second is that they may not be dependent upon others for their support: "That ye may walk becomingly toward them that are without, and may have need of nothing." True "love of the brethren" will incline one to seek peace, to attend to his own task, and to maintain an honest independence.

C. COMFORT CONCERNING THE DEAD
Ch. 4:13-18

13 But we would not have you ignorant, brethren, concerning them that fall asleep; that ye sorrow not, even as the rest, who have no hope. 14 For if we believe that Jesus died and rose again, even so them also that are fallen asleep in Jesus will God bring with him. 15 For this we say unto you by the word of the Lord, that we that are alive, that are left unto the coming of the Lord, shall in no wise precede them that are fallen asleep. 16 For the Lord himself shall descend from heaven, with a shout, with the voice of the archangel, and with the trump of God: and the dead in Christ shall rise first; 17 then we that are alive, that are left, shall together with them be caught up in the clouds, to meet the Lord in the air: and so shall we ever be with the Lord. 18 Wherefore comfort one another with these words.

Is the soul immortal?   Will personality persist after death?   "If a man die, shall he live again?"   Shall we recognize our friends in heaven?   These questions ever have been of supreme interest to the human heart.   To these questions Christ had given an affirmative reply, on which imperishable and inspiring beliefs are firmly founded. There were, however, more specific yet related questions which had arisen among the Christians at Thessalonica: Would those who were alive when the Lord returned have an advantage over those who should die before that event? What would be the experience or fate of the latter?   Would they share in the glory of that great day?

As to the personal return of Christ there was not the slightest doubt. The belief in that return was an essential article of the faith of the Thessalonians. They are described as those who "turned unto God from idols, to serve a living and true God, and to wait for his Son from heaven." So real and possibly so near did they regard this return that some had abandoned their daily tasks, and were living in idle and feverish expectation, depending on their brethren for support. It was this situation which Paul discussed in the previous paragraph. Possibly it led him next to consider this problem in connection with the coming of Christ. The question had been brought to him by Timothy, or sent to him directly by the Thessalonians.

Paul's reply is practical. He does not review the matter at length. He says only enough to enforce an exhortation to comfort. This portion of his letter was not intended so much to impart instruction as to give encouragement and to direct a course of life. Nevertheless, the statements are of priceless value. The paragraph is the most interesting and important of the whole epistle.

Paul acknowledges the seriousness of the subject by his opening phrase, "We would not have you ignorant." These words are frequently employed to introduce a matter of great weight. Here Paul is to write "concerning them that fall asleep," that is, asleep in death. The readers had possibly thought that they all would live to welcome the returning Christ. Unexpectedly one after another of their friends was meeting death. Their own hearts were torn not only by bereavement but by the fear that they might never see their friends again; by the fear, also, that these friends might miss the blessedness that they themselves were soon to enjoy.

Paul undertakes to show them why they should entertain no such fear for these friends; they should "sorrow not, even as the rest, who have no hope." Aside from Christians, other mourners in Thessalonica had no expec-

tation of reunion with their friends who had died. To this
present day nothing is more pitiful than the hopelessness
of the pagan world in the face of death.

The Christian believes not only in a future life but also
that by a glorious resurrection the immortal soul will be
clothed with a deathless body. This belief is based upon
the resurrection of Christ, which was a proof and a type
of the resurrection of his followers: "For if we believe that
Jesus died and rose again, even so them also that are fallen
asleep in Jesus will God bring with him."

The meaning is quite clear. Those who die with faith
in Christ will be with him and will be brought back with
him out of the sphere of the unseen, when he appears.
One phrase, however, is difficult to translate. It has become so precious to readers of the English Bible that it
should be treated with a certain reverence and reserve.
"Asleep in Jesus" is literally "asleep through Jesus." It
may mean that, because of their relation to him, death
has lost its terror for Christians. It is simply falling asleep;
and sleep is restful, sleep is refreshing, sleep implies awak-
ing and dawn. For a believer, death is simply to have the
Master lull him to sleep as a mother hushes her child to
slumber.

This expression, however, is so unusual and surprising
that most modern translators prefer to change the order
of the words and to read, "Them also that are fallen asleep
will God through Jesus bring with him." This would draw
attention to a fact which Paul frequently states, namely,
that the resurrection of believers will be wrought by the
power of Christ. In virtue of his resurrection, and because
he is the Savior and Redeemer, he will bring back in the
fullness of immortal life those who for a time have "fallen
asleep" in death.

Whichever translation is preferred, it is interesting to
note that this is the first mention, in all literature, of the
resurrection of Christ. Paul must have written the words
within twenty years after that event. It was thus a cardi-

nal doctrine of primitive Christianity, and with it was associated the belief in the resurrection of the followers of Christ.

About this resurrection Paul now continues to speak. He touches upon the particular point which concerned his readers. He assures them that, far from missing the blessedness attending the return of the Lord, believers who had died will be the first to share in that blessedness. "This we say unto you by the word of the Lord," writes the apostle, intimating that his message is in substance a divine revelation. "We that are alive, that are left unto the coming of the Lord, shall in no wise precede them that are fallen asleep." The order of events is to be as follows: "The Lord himself shall descend from heaven, with a shout, with the voice of the archangel, and with the trump of God: and the dead in Christ shall rise first; then we that are alive, that are left, shall together with them be caught up in the clouds, to meet the Lord in the air."

Paul thought that he might live to see the Lord return. He never asserted that he would or that he would not. To make either assertion would be to assume a position against which he warns his followers in the paragraph which follows. Sometimes, as here, he identifies himself with those who will be alive when Christ returns. Frequently, as in II Cor. 4:14; 5:1, he identifies himself with those who will rise from the dead when Christ returns. His attitude is that of all true Christians in every age. We should look for the coming of our Lord as an event the time of which is absolutely unknown, an event which may occur in any generation.

The special word of instruction is that in the great drama of the returning Christ the very first act will be the resurrection of the dead. As to the exact nature of that glorious return it is useless to speculate. One cannot tell just what is meant by the "shout," the "voice," the "trump." We are assured, however, that when Christ does appear, then will occur the resurrection of dead believers. The next act will be the rapture of the living. As to the previous state of the blessed dead, the resurrection body, or the transformation of the living, nothing is said here. The nature of that body and of that miraculous change is considered in I Cor., ch. 15. Here the thought is centered upon the reunion of those who have gone to be with Christ and of those who are living when Christ returns. They will meet "in the air." More important still, they will "meet the Lord in the air."

The reserve and restraint of the apostle are remarkable. He speaks in figures which he does not interpret, nor does he let his imagination play upon details which must have been alluring. He sums up the whole message of blessedness and glory, not by descriptions of physical or material splendor, but in one great spiritual reality: "So shall we ever be with the Lord." This is the great consummation. This is the realization of our highest hopes, to be "together" and to be "with the Lord," forever and forever.

There is far too little here to satisfy our curiosity. A hundred questions come to mind to which no answer is given. But there is enough here to give courage and consolation, even in "the valley of the shadow of death." Therefore, Paul can express thus the real purpose of his message: "Wherefore comfort one another with these words."

D. ENCOURAGEMENT TO WATCHFULNESS
Ch. 5:1-11

1 But concerning the times and the seasons, brethren, ye have no need that aught be written unto you. 2 For yourselves know perfectly that the day of the Lord so cometh as a thief in the night. 3 When they are saying, Peace and safety, then sudden destruction cometh upon them, as travail upon a woman with child; and they shall in no wise escape. 4 But ye, brethren, are not in darkness, that that day should overtake you as a thief: 5 for ye are all sons of light, and sons of the day: we are not of the night, nor

*of darkness; 6 so then let us not sleep, as do the rest, but
let us watch and be sober. 7 For they that sleep sleep in
the night; and they that are drunken are drunken in the
night. 8 But let us, since we are of the day, be sober, putting on the breastplate of faith and love; and for a helmet,
the hope of salvation. 9 For God appointed us not unto
wrath, but unto the obtaining of salvation through our
Lord Jesus Christ, 10 who died for us, that, whether we
wake or sleep, we should live together with him.   11
Wherefore exhort one another, and build each other up,
even as also ye do.*

There are two wrong attitudes of mind toward our
Lord's return. One is that of feverish expectation. The
other is that of cold indifference and careless neglect.
Both had been manifested at Thessalonica. Both are common today. The first may result in fanaticism, and in confusing the truth with fantastic creations of fancy. The
second may encourage a life of worldly and sensual indul-
gence. To guard against both these errors Paul exhorts
his readers to be calm and to be watchful.

Evidently the Thessalonians were eager to receive more
definite instruction as to the time of Christ's coming.
Some thought it so near that daily work was no longer
necessary. Some feared that if it were delayed, death
would rob them of their friends. Paul assures them that
the time is unknown. He feels that they do not need instruction so much as encouragement. Thus he exhorts
them to keep vigil, to watch and wait and hope.

"But concerning the times and the seasons, brethren"
—the periods of time and the exact character of the epochs
to intervene before the return of Christ—"ye have no
need that aught be written unto you." There was "no
need," not because these times and seasons were known,
but because he had previously taught them that the time
never had been revealed. "Yourselves know perfectly that
the day of the Lord so cometh as a thief in the night."
"The day of the Lord" means "the day of Christ's return."

It will be as unexpected and surprising as the entrance into a home of a thief by night.

However, the surprise will be for the unbelieving world rather than for Christians. The latter are supposed to be awake and on the watch. This is not so with unbelievers: "When they are saying, Peace and safety, then sudden destruction cometh upon them."

This false sense of security preceding his return was pictured by our Lord. As in the days of Noah, immediately before the divine judgment fell, men were buying and selling, "marrying and giving in marriage," so just before his return men will be following their usual course of life when the dread event will overwhelm them "and they shall in no wise escape."

This return of Christ does have its solemn punitive phase of judgment upon the impenitent and the godless. For the believer it is the time of deliverance. It is the day of his perfected salvation. For him the coming of Christ should not be a sudden and overwhelming surprise. Certain signs are to be given, certain events to immediately precede. Of these Paul will write in his next epistle. Christians should be looking for Christ's return and living lives of such sobriety and purity that the approach of the great day will give them no consternation, no fear: "Ye, brethren, are not in darkness, that that day should overtake you as a thief: for ye are all sons of light, and sons of the day." "Darkness" here indicates "ignorance." However, as the following sentences show, it has a further intimation of moral depravity. Christians are "sons of light." They possess knowledge of Christ's return, in striking contrast with the benighted state of the unbelieving world, Christians are "sons of the day," particularly of the day of Christ's return. For that day they are waiting, and in its dawning they will rejoice.

Since, then, "we are not of the night, nor of darkness"—or, inasmuch as we Christians, the writers as well as the readers, are not ignorant of Christ's return—"so then let us not sleep, as do the rest." Here "sleep" denotes the careless indifference which would be startled by the unexpected coming of Christ. "Let us watch and be sober." It is the duty of a Christian to be vigilant. He is not to be excited and distracted but to be "sober," calm and collected, in view of the Lord's return.

In contrast with this rightful attitude of the Christian, men of the world are spending the night in two ways, neither of which is appropriate to the day. Either they are asleep, utterly indifferent to the coming judgment, or they are indulging in drunken revelry, excited and interested indeed, but absorbed in what is base and unworthy.

In striking contrast to such conduct is the exhortation addressed to Christians: "Let us, since we are of the day, be sober, putting on the breastplate of faith and love; and for a helmet, the hope of salvation." Thus suddenly the figure changes. The Christian is to be not only vigilant and calm, but as a soldier he is to be armed and ready for spiritual conflict, while waiting for the coming of Christ. Here the armor described is composed of "faith" and "love" and "hope." In the opening of this epistle mention is made of this familiar triad of virtues. There they are viewed as forces, each producing its characteristic effect in Christian life, the "work of faith and labor of love and patience of hope." Here they are means of protection against the assaults of moral evil.

It is the "helmet, the hope of salvation," upon which Paul's thought continues to dwell. The coming of Christ and the deliverance he will bring is the essential message of the epistle. That hope is the safeguard against carelessness or despair. It is certain to give victory in the time of conflict.

For the Christian the divine purpose is not condemnation but glory and blessedness: "For God appointed us not unto wrath, but unto the obtaining of salvation through our Lord Jesus Christ."

This salvation has been wrought through the redeeming work of Christ, "who died for us." The ultimate purpose of this death, the object of his sacrifice, was that Christ might bring us into union with himself. "That, whether we wake or sleep"—whether, at his coming, we "are keeping vigil in life or are sleeping in death"—"we should live together with him," for this future life of fellowship with Christ, which will be perfected at his appearance, is the climax and consummation of our Christian hope. "Wherefore," concludes the apostle, "exhort one another, and build each other up, even as also ye do." The admonition is based on the truths of which he has been writing. He is saying, in effect: "Since Christ is coming, since his return is your bright and blessed hope, since he gives power to live lives worthy of such a hope, since he grants you assurance of your salvation and future glory, therefore, comfort one another and strengthen one another by cherishing and rehearsing these inspiring truths. Such is indeed your practice. See that you do so more and more."

E. FINAL EXHORTATIONS
Ch. 5:12-22

12 But we beseech you, brethren, to know them that labor among you, and are over you in the Lord, and admonish you; 13 and to esteem them exceeding highly in love for their work's sake. Be at peace among yourselves. 14 And we exhort you, brethren, admonish the disorderly, encourage the fainthearted, support the weak, be longsuffering toward all. 15 See that none render unto any one evil for evil; but always follow after that which is good, one toward another, and toward all. 16 Rejoice always; 17 pray without ceasing; 18 in everything give thanks: for this is the will of God in Christ Jesus to you-ward. 19 Quench not the Spirit; 20 despise not prophesyings; 21 prove all things; hold fast that which is good; 22 abstain from every form of evil.

In the practical portion of the epistle (chs. 4; 5), the apostle has enjoined upon his readers to be pure and loving, to comfort one another, and to be watchful in view of the Lord's return. He now gives a series of closing exhortations. These are not closely connected. The first relates to church leaders. The second concerns the disorderly and fainthearted. The third group relates to the general character of Christian life, and the last to the exercise of spirtual gifts.

"But we beseech you, brethren"—this indicates that the writer is turning to enforce a new line of Christian duty— "to know them that labor among you." "To know" here means "to know in their true character," "to respect," "to appreciate worth." "Them that labor among you" refers to the officers of the church. Evidently the form of church organization was very simple, but it did exist. Even in that primitive Christian society there were persons whom the apostles could designate as "them that labor among you, and are over you in the Lord, and admonish you."

These three clauses are not to be interpreted as designating three classes of officers. They rather indicate three aspects or forms of the service which the church leaders were rendering. "Labor" indicates toil and wearisome effort. Official position was no empty honor; it implied self-denying work. "Them that . . . are over you in the Lord" does not define an office but points to guidance in spiritual matters, or in all the concerns and activities of the church. "Them that . . . admonish you" describes the leaders as performing the task of brotherly warning and kindly counsel.

Such leaders are to be esteemed "exceeding highly in love for their work's sake." They are to be regarded with warm affection. This love and honor should be shown not in respect for an office, but in view of the importance of the work and the fidelity with which it is being done.

Such an attitude of respect and honor and love toward the leaders of the church would result in a spirit of peace in the Christian community. Thus the exhortation, "Be at peace among yourselves," is not unrelated to the exhortation which precedes, while it does turn the thought from the officers to the members of the church and reminds them of the necessity of holding one another in similar esteem and love.

Indeed, it is to the mutual obligations of church members that the following exhortations specifically refer. It is not enough to respect those who are leaders in the church, to refrain from criticizing them, or to honor them for the work they are called to do. All Christians must help them and share in their labors. The presence in the church of faithful officers relieves no member from definite responsibility for the spiritual welfare of his fellow believers. Especially heavy is the responsibility of those who regard themselves as strong and mature in the Christian life.

"We exhort you, brethren," writes the apostle—and the exhortation is thus addressed to each one in the community of believers—"admonish the disorderly." "Those who do not keep in the ranks" is the literal meaning of "disorderly." It probably refers specifically to those who were abandoning their tasks and duties because of a feverish expectation of the immediate return of Christ. It may include all who are idle, meddlesome, and of unquiet mind. Such must be warned, rebuked, admonished, by their Christian brethren.

In real contrast there are "the fainthearted": those who have lost courage; those who are anxious about the dead, or about their own salvation; those who are despondent or in despair. There are many such. It is the duty of fellow Christians not to despise but to "encourage" them, to give them sympathy and cheer. "Support the weak"—not those lacking in physical strength, not those in need of material relief, but those who are morally and spiritually weak, those who are about to yield to temptation, those who cannot endure the testing of persecution and reproach. To them support and aid must be given.

"Be longsuffering toward all." Patience must be shown toward the erring, the despondent, the weak—indeed, toward all men. Christians are not to be of hasty temper. They are to be characterized by love, and love "beareth all things, believeth all things, hopeth all things, endureth all things. Love never faileth."

The Christian, therefore, can harbor no spirit of revenge. He must endeavor also, as far as possible, to check that spirit in others, and to seek the highest good and continuous welfare of all: "See that none render unto any one evil for evil; but always follow after that which is good, one toward another, and toward all."

The three exhortations which follow have been called "the standing orders of the Christian church," for, no matter what the circumstances may be, these commands are at all times in force: "Rejoice always; pray without ceasing; in everything give thanks." The injunction always to be joyful has been called "essentially Christian," since Christianity is based upon "glad tidings"; "characteristically Pauline," since joy was his constant experience and "Rejoice" his repeated command; and "specifically appropriate," since the Thessalonians were sorrowing beyond necessity, yet suffering real bereavement and distress. However, Paul was no shallow optimist. He knew that pain and loss are real. He means, however, that amidst and beneath unquestioned sorrows there can exist unfailing springs of joy. He indicates that the cultivation of a spirit of constant gladness is a Christian duty.

"Pray without ceasing." To obey this command would enable one to "rejoice always." It is, however, a distinct injunction. It is not to be unduly pressed. It does not mean the abandonment of tasks and duties and times of rest, and the devotion of life to the one exercise of communion with God. Nor yet is it to be minimized to mean merely that one should cultivate a habit of prayer. Life should be lived in the continual spirit of worship. "Beneath the stream of thought there should flow the deep current of unconscious communion with God and the sense of his presence, a current ever and again rising into conscious petition and adoration and praise."

One who thus lives will naturally and necessarily obey the command, "In everything give thanks." This is not only to express gratitude for everything, although that should be done, but also to "give thanks" under all conditions and in all circumstances.

Obedience to these commands is difficult. Indeed, it may seem impossible. However, a ringing word of encouragement is added: "This is the will of God in Christ Jesus to you-ward." That we should lead lives of continual joy, of ceaseless prayer, of constant thanksgiving, is not merely the desire, the expectation, the command of God; it is his purpose, his will, and therefore is certain to be fulfilled. This ideal has been realized in Christ, and it is in his power, and in virtue of his indwelling, that such an ideal will be realized with increasing perfection by those who trust and follow him.

"Quench not the Spirit." There is a real sense in which any Christian may quench the Spirit. One may do so when in any way he refuses the guidance or represses the impulses, or neglects to use the gifts or to cultivate the graces, of the Spirit. All should welcome God's Spirit and should seek to be sensitive to his every breathing in our hearts. However, as used here, the warning is more specific and the message more limited. The words which follow, "Despise not prophesying," have led to the conclusion that the word "Spirit" refers here to those unique spiritual gifts which were granted to the early church. These were temporary and were miraculous in character. They included "tongues," "prophecy," "interpretation of tongues," gifts of "healing." These gifts were usually manifested in the public gathering of Christians. Their exercise was open to abuse. In some cases it led to disorder, to confusion, even to disgrace. The result was that in some quarters these gifts fell into disrepute. Christians were tempted to repress the movings of the Spirit in their own hearts, and to restrain others who would have been helpful in the use of their divine endowments.

The gift of prophecy in particular was treated lightly, neglected, possibly ridiculed. By "prophesyings" was meant not only predictions but all divine messages mediated by the Spirit. With his usual sanity Paul maintains a right balance. Whatever abuses may have existed, he warns his readers against underrating the gifts of the Spirit, and opposing his influences: "Quench not the Spirit; despise not prophesyings." But he recognizes the danger of extravagance, of spurious utterances, of counterfeit miracles, of false prophecies; and he urges his readers to "prove all things" and to "hold fast that which is good." The tests to be applied he does not specify. Elsewhere he indicates that all spiritual gifts are to be exercised in love, that their real purpose must be to edify others, and that those who are really moved by the Spirit will admit the Lordship of Christ and will endeavor to advance his glory.

"Abstain from every form of evil" is probably a general exhortation referring to all spheres of life and experience. Some readers, however, connect it with what has gone before and understand it to mean: "Test all prophecies, accept those which are real and genuine, reject all which are false or which are not uttered in love and do not tend to strengthen and upbuild the church." It may be best to accept this closing exhortation, however, as being broad and inclusive, urging upon Christians conduct free from fault and reproach.

F. CONCLUSION   Ch. 5:23-28

23 And the God of peace himself sanctify you wholly; and may your spirit and soul and body be preserved entire, without blame at the coming of our Lord Jesus Christ. 24 Faithful is he that calleth you, who will also do it.

25 Brethren, pray for us.

26 Salute all the brethren with a holy kiss. 27 I adjure you by the Lord that this epistle be read unto all the brethren.

28 The grace of our Lord Jesus Christ be with you.

From exhortation Paul now turns to prayer. This is quite in accord with his own precepts and practice. He would have his readers "rejoice always; pray without ceasing," and "in everything give thanks." So this epistle has been in large measure an expression of joyful praise; and now when the writer has given a few sentences of practical advice, realizing that all human effort is futile without divine aid, he turns to God in earnest petition. The prayer is addressed to "the God of peace." The meaning is "the God who is the Source of peace." This is in possible contrast to those breaches of harmony produced by the moral faults against which the readers have now been warned. "Peace," however, may be regarded as the chief, or even as the sum, of all divine gifts and bestowals. Thus interpreted, God is here addressed as "the Giver of all spiritual grace and blessings."

The prayer, in substance, is that the readers may be kept perfect until the return of Christ: "The God of peace himself sanctify you wholly." "Himself" indicates that God, and God alone, can so sanctify. This sanctification is not only an act but a process. To sanctify is to set aside or to separate for the service of God, to consecrate but also to purify, to make fit for such service and to free from all fault. The prayer is that this may be done "wholly," that is, "throughout" or "through and through."

This complete sanctification is described even more fully: "And may your spirit and soul and body be preserved entire, without blame." It need not be supposed that Paul is here giving a scientific and technical division of the component parts of human nature. "Spirit" and "soul" are not to be regarded as absolutely separate and distinct elements. The reference is to the one indivisible personality, in its Godward relations, in its natural activities, and in its uses of the body. The prayer is that every aspect of one's life, every expression of the inner self, every aspiration and motive, as well as all forms of conduct, shall be sanctified. The entire being is to be "preserved" as an undivided whole, intact, "entire." The purpose is that

believers may be found "without blame at the coming of
our Lord Jesus Christ." The return of Christ is mentioned as the time when true character will be revealed
and also when perfection will be complete.

That even so extraordinary a prayer will be answered is
affirmed by the words at its close: "Faithful is he that
calleth you, who will also do it." That believers might become holy, sanctified, complete, was the very purpose of
God in calling them into the fellowship of his Son. It is
absolutely certain, therefore, that this purpose will be
realized. The ultimate moral perfection of the Thessalonians is said to depend not only upon their own efforts
or upon the prayers of the apostle, but upon the promises
and the unfailing power of God.

Having thus prayed for his readers, the apostle now
asks them to pray for him and for his fellow workers:
"Brethren, pray for us." Repeatedly in his epistles does
Paul record this request. Yet the words are never an
empty form, never a mere pious greeting.

The great apostle longed to be remembered by his
friends. His heart was hungry for their sympathy. Great
missionary to the Gentile world as he was, he believed that
the intercession of these converted pagans would help him
in his service and strengthen him for his task.

"Salute all the brethren with a holy kiss." There is no
sufficient reason to suppose that this exhortation was addressed only to the elders or the officers of the church; nor
yet that it referred to men alone. The kiss was a familiar
form of salutation among Orientals. It quite usually was
employed by members of a family in greeting one another.
The custom among early Christians indicated their belief
that the church of Christ formed a real brotherhood. The
reference here undoubtedly is to the "holy kiss," the Christian salutation, the expression of friendship and religious
fellowship.

The last of the three closing exhortations is peculiarly
solemn in its form: "I adjure you by the Lord that this

epistle be read unto all the brethren." The apostle thus insists that it be read in the public assembly of the entire congregation. Exactly the motive for so emphatic an injunction is not known. It need, however, occasion no wonder or surprise. The letter was of great importance. Many needed its comfort. Others needed its guidance. All would rejoice in its cheer, its message of affection and of hope.

This was the first book of the New Testament to be written. Little did the apostle know of all the priceless contents of that volume, the very creation of which he could not have anticipated. Yet his closing exhortation intimates to us the propriety of such public reading of Paul's epistles, and encourages us to believe that they were written, not for one class or group alone, but for all the members "of the household of the faith."

In place of the word of farewell with which letters of the day usually closed is the apostolic benediction in its briefest form. It is an invocation of "grace"—a word found at the close of every epistle written by Paul—the boundless unmerited favor of God revealed and mediated through Christ.

"The grace of our Lord Jesus Christ be with you."

THE SECOND EPISTLE OF PAUL
TO THE THESSALONIANS

THE OUTLINE

A. SALUTATION II Thess. 1:1-2

1 Paul, and Silvanus, and Timothy, unto the church of the Thessalonians in God our Father and the Lord Jesus Christ; 2 Grace to you and peace from God the Father and the Lord Jesus Christ.

In the opening lines of the letter, Paul unites his name with that of his missionary companions in expressing to the Christians of Thessalonica his prayer for divine grace and peace. Paul was still at Corinth. Only a few months had elapsed since the dispatch of his First Epistle to the Thessalonians. Evidently conditions had not improved. The persecution of the church had increased. Misunderstanding as to the time of the Second Advent had become more serious. Expectation of the immediate return of Christ had led larger numbers of Christians to live in idleness and disorder. Thus, while the main message of this letter consists of instruction as to the time of the return of Christ, the opening chapter contains consolation for those in distress and the closing chapter conveys exhortations concerning those in need of discipline.

The salutation with which the epistle begins is in the form which was usual in letters of the day. It introduces the writer and the readers, and contains a greeting in the form of a wish or prayer. It is in the exact form of the salutation with which the First Epistle is begun, the only changes being that "God the Father" is altered to "God our Father," while "grace" and "peace" are traced to their origin in "God the Father and the Lord Jesus Christ."

In again uniting his name with those of Silvanus and Timothy, Paul does not intend to indicate that he is not the actual author of the epistle. He wishes, however, to show courtesy to his associates, and to strengthen the force of his message. He indicates that these companions know and endorse what the letter contains. He is certain, also, that their names are dear to the hearts of his readers and that the mention of them will assure an even more eager reception for his words.

Silvanus, known in The Acts by the shorter name of Silas, was a man of prominence in the early church. He was called a "prophet," that is, an inspired teacher. Like Paul he possessed Roman citizenship. He was one of the "chief men among the brethren" in Judea who were commissioned, with Paul and Barnabas, to convey to Antioch the decree of the Council at Jerusalem. When Paul and Barnabas had separated because of their difference of opinion concerning John Mark, Silas was chosen to take the place of Barnabas on Paul's second missionary journey. On reaching Lystra they were joined by a young convert named Timothy. His father was a Greek, his mother a Jewess. He had been baptized by Paul, probably on Paul's first missionary journey. He became the most constant and best-loved companion of the apostle. Both Silvanus and Timothy, therefore, were with Paul on this second missionary journey, which brought them to Europe, and so to Philippi, to Thessalonica, to Athens, and to Corinth. From Athens they had been sent back by Paul to Thessalonica. It was after they had rejoined Paul at Corinth that his letters were written to the Thessalonian church.

In the welfare of that church Paul felt a deep concern. This was due not only to his tender interest in his converts, but also because of the importance of their city as a missionary center. It was on the main highway from Rome to the East. It was the outlet for a fertile district and had easy access to the sea. It was a free city with special privileges and powers.   Consequently, it was a prominent military and commercial center.   In this city so strategically located, in this metropolis with its rushing tides of life and its pagan cults, Paul and his friends succeeded in establishing so strong a Christian church that, even when writing his First Epistle, Paul could assert that through it Macedonia and Achaia had been evangelized and the gospel had been carried to the regions beyond.

Here Paul describes the church as being "in God our Father and the Lord Jesus Christ."   The change from "the Father" to "our Father" indicates that it is the divine Fatherhood in relation to man and not to Christ that is particularly in Paul's mind.   The immediate addition of the words "the Lord Jesus Christ" indicates that here the term is used of Christians rather than of mankind at large. These Christians are enabled by the Spirit of the Son to call God "Abba, Father."   It is noticeable that in these earliest of Paul's epistles he intimates an equality between the Father and the Son.

The phrases applied to the church indicate that it is a spiritual body, distinct from any mere political or social organization.   The word translated "church" means an "assembly," a body of men "called out."   Hence in its sacred use it may be regarded as indicating an assembly of believers called out from the world by the Spirit of God and yielding to the Lordship of the Son of God.   This church in Thessalonica is "in God" and in Christ.   That is to say, all that the church is, all that for which it exists, all that it seeks to do, is vitally related to God as the divine Father and to Jesus Christ as its divine Savior and Lord.

To this church Paul and his companions send the greeting, "Grace to you and peace from God the Father and the Lord Jesus Christ."   Because this greeting is familiar it must not be allowed to lose its force.   It is the wish or the prayer of the apostle that a twofold blessing may come to his readers from a twofold source.   "Grace" is the unmerited love of God revealed and communicated by Christ.

"Peace" is the inner tranquillity of soul made possible for believers by faith in Christ. Together they may be regarded as the sum of all spiritual good. In the First Epistle this greeting stands in its simplest form: "Grace to you and peace." Here these two gifts are traced to their divine origin—to "God the Father and the Lord Jesus Christ." There is no better prayer to offer for our friends, there is no more noble desire to cherish for ourselves, than a fuller bestowal of divine grace and a deeper experience of "the peace . . . , which passeth all understanding."

B. THANKSGIVING Ch. 1:3-10

3 We are bound to give thanks to God always for you, brethren, even as it is meet, for that your faith groweth exceedingly, and the love of each one of you all toward one another aboundeth; 4 so that we ourselves glory in you in the churches of God for your patience and faith in all your persecutions and in the afflictions which ye endure; 5 which is a manifest token of the righteous judgment of God; to the end that ye may be counted worthy of the kingdom of God, for which ye also suffer: 6 if so be that it is a righteous thing with God to recompense affliction to them that afflict you, 7 and to you that are afflicted rest with us, at the revelation of the Lord Jesus from heaven with the angels of his power in flaming fire, 8 rendering vengeance to them that know not God, and to them that obey not the gospel of our Lord Jesus: 9 who shall suffer punishment, even eternal destruction from the face of the Lord and from the glory of his might, 10 when he shall come to be glorified in his saints, and to be marvelled at in all them that believed (because our testimony unto you was believed) in that day.

Quite commonly Paul follows his salutation with a thanksgiving. Usually his gratitude is in view of certain virtues possessed by those to whom he writes. The virtues are frequently those that form the familiar triad of faith and hope and love. These cardinal Christian graces

are those that are mentioned in the thanksgiving at the
opening of the First Epistle to the Thessalonians: "Your
work of faith and labor of love and patience of hope."   In
this thanksgiving special mention is made of faith and love
and patience.   Yet this patience is in view of the return
of Christ, which is the supreme object and the highest form
of hope.   Indeed, as Paul dwells upon this "revelation of
the Lord Jesus from heaven," his thanksgiving melts into
a great message of cheer, intended to encourage those
whose patience is being tested by a present experience of
bitter persecution.

While the customary thanksgiving is in substance similar to that of the First Epistle, it does contain certain dis-
tinctive features.   It points to the progress of the Thessalonians' faith and love, and states the consequent boasting
of Paul on their behalf.   Then, too, the expression here is
more emphatic.   Not only does Paul "give thanks to God,"
but he adds, "We are bound" so to do.   It is a duty as well
as a privilege.   For all the benefits and blessings we receive, thanksgiving is an actual debt which we owe to
God.   It is a personal obligation resting upon us.   "Even
as it is meet," writes Paul, indicating that such thanksgiving is due, not only because of the goodness of God, but
because of the merit of the Thessalonians.   Their conduct
warrants such gratitude.

"Your faith groweth exceedingly," the apostle declares,
"and the love of each one of you all toward one another
aboundeth."   As to their faith, Paul earlier seems to have
felt some anxiety, and he had written his First Epistle
partly to remedy what was "lacking" in their faith.   Now
he is returning thanks that this faith is having what he
describes as an "exuberant growth."   So, too, their love
is characterized as manifest not only to individuals but to
the entire body of believers.   Such unlimited and abounding love was in answer to the prayer voiced by Paul in his
previous letter, "The Lord make you to increase and
abound in love one toward another, and toward all men."

It is notable that Paul acknowledges these Christian graces as characterizing a church where there exists so much imperfection. He is about to mention and to rebuke the ignorance and deception and fanaticism and disorder which have been reported. However, he is not of those who are blinded to the virtues by the faults of their fellow Christians. Some love to discover and to condemn moral weakness in others. It affords them at no expense the delightful feeling of conscious superiority.

It is also to be observed that Paul does not congratulate his readers; he gives thanks to God. He traces the manifest virtues to their source in divine grace. Furthermore, Paul is not only thankful; he is boastful. He feels a pardonable pride in the spiritual growth of his converts: "We ourselves glory in you in the churches of God." The particular ground of Paul's boasting is their "patience and faith" in all the "persecutions and . . . afflictions" which they are enduring. "Patience" denotes "steadfast endurance." "Persecutions" indicates the hostile attacks of their enemies. "Afflictions" points to any or to consequent sufferings or tribulations. "Patience" is here associated with "faith," its real source. So then their faith amid affliction is the substance of the apostle's boast as he reports their triumph to the churches of Achaia and of the more distant regions with which he is in communication.

Such steadfast faith Paul declares to be "a manifest token of the righteous judgment of God." That is to say, their heroic endurance is so unusual as to indicate its divine source. God must be on their side. Therefore, they are sure to be delivered, and their enemies are certain to be punished, since justice is justice and God is God. Of this future deliverance and punishment their present patience is a "token," or proof. It cannot but result in their being "counted worthy of the kingdom of God." The particular reference here is to the future glorious aspect of that Kingdom. The issue of faith, by which earthly sufferings are endured, is not only the development of spiritual virtues, but the inheritance of heavenly blessedness: "For which ye also suffer." Such a belief and hope has been the proper stay and comfort of sufferers through all the Christian centuries.

This reward of the righteous is one aspect of the divine judgment. There is another: the wicked are to be punished, inasmuch, or since, "it is a righteous thing with God to recompense affliction to them that afflict you, and to you that are afflicted rest with us." Such reasoning follows the simplest axiom of divine justice. Retribution is inevitable. Sin and suffering are inseparable. In time or in eternity "whatsoever a man soweth, that shall he also reap." The persecutor is certain of punishment; the innocent sufferer is assured of vindication, of "rest," of relief. In that future deliverance Paul and his companions are certain to be associated with the readers. "You that are afflicted" are to have "rest with us," writes the apostle. He is certain that if they have suffered together, they also will be glorified together.

The time of this deliverance is to be "at the revelation of the Lord Jesus from heaven with the angels of his power in flaming fire." The "rest" comes when Christ comes. It is not that "sleep" of death to which Jesus referred when his friend Lazarus died. Nor is the expression the same as that "sabbath rest" which remains "for the people of God" (Heb. 4:9). This deliverance begins when they are "caught up [together] in the clouds, to meet the Lord in the air" (I Thess. 4:17). Such a deliverance was not granted to the readers of this letter. They did "fall asleep." However, they are to share with all believers in the glory and blessedness of "the revelation of the Lord Jesus," when he comes to give rest to those who are suffering for his sake.

It is evident that Paul mentions no interval between the time of deliverance and the time of retribution. No period of years elapses. The "rest" and the "destruction" follow in quick succession.

Christ is pictured as the Agent who exacts the penalty, "rendering vengeance." These last words must not imply "taking revenge." There can be nothing vindictive in the thought or act of God. It is, however, a solemn infliction of justice that is here described. Divine retribution is absolutely inevitable.

This "vengeance" is to be rendered "to them that know not God, and to them that obey not the gospel of our Lord Jesus." It is not necessary to suppose that Paul here describes two distinct classes of men, as for example Gentiles and Jews. Rather he includes all who are willfully ignorant of God and stubbornly refuse the gospel of his Son. Paul does not mean that men will be held responsible for not believing truths of which they never have been told, nor for ignorance of a gospel which they have not heard. Those he has in mind are such as disobey the light of nature and of conscience, and such as refuse the gospel call to repentance and faith. Enemies of purity and truth and love, malignant persecutors of Christ and his followers—these are the offenders upon whom the penalty must fall.

This penalty is described as "eternal destruction from the face of the Lord and from the glory of his might." These words must be read with sadness, even with trembling. The attempt to evade their meaning or to weaken their force is futile. The duration of the punishment is unlimited. Its nature is not annihilation but banishment from the presence of God. It is exclusion from the future "vision beatific" enjoyed by those who "shall see God," who "shall see his face," who shall enjoy his fellowship and his favor. Those thus excluded shall not behold "the glory of his might," the splendor radiating from the manifested power of God.

There is another very different aspect of the return of Christ. He comes not only to punish and to destroy. "He shall come," writes the apostle, "to be glorified in his saints, and to be marvelled at in all them that believed."

"Saints" is the common and inclusive term for all Christians. In and through them the glory of their Lord will be revealed. Even now the grace and power of Christ are manifested in the lives of his true followers. However, when Christ again appears, his followers will "appear with him in glory," and all their perfection of character, all the blessedness of their condition, will be but an outshining, a marvelous exhibition, of his power and goodness and grace.

Among these saints the Thessalonians would be numbered, for Paul adds, "Because our testimony unto you was believed." Their rest from present persecution, their share in future glory were indeed grounds for gratitude. Therefore, the long statement as to the punishment of their persecutors must not make the reader forget that we still are here reading a part of the thanksgiving with which the epistle opens. However, the instruction concerning the return of Christ is not a mere parenthesis in this opening paragraph of praise. It touches the very heart of the message. Paul is writing concerning the Second Coming of Christ. This first chapter introduces his subject and deals with the Advent in relation to present suffering. The second chapter considers the Advent in relation to the "man of sin." The last chapter, in view of this Advent, deals with the daily duty of those whose hope is fixed upon Christ.

C. PRAYER   Ch. 1:11-12

11 To which end we also pray always for you, that our God may count you worthy of your calling, and fulfil every desire of goodness and every work of faith, with power; 12 that the name of our Lord Jesus may be glorified in you, and ye in him, according to the grace of our God and the Lord Jesus Christ.

It is the custom of Paul to open his epistles with a greeting, a thanksgiving, and a prayer. These apostolic prayers

form some of the most precious portions of his letters.
Quite commonly they are closely entwined with the expressions of thanks which precede. In some cases they
melt into the main currents of the epistles which follow.
In the Second Epistle to the Thessalonians, the opening
thanksgiving has reached its climax in a reference to the
radiant glories attending the Second Coming of Christ.
Then it is that innocent sufferers shall be delivered from
their tormentors and loyal believers shall be granted a
share in the glory of their returning Lord. Therefore Paul
prays that his readers may experience such moral and
spiritual growth that they may be accounted worthy to
partake in this future blessedness and may ever reflect
credit upon the name of Christ.

"To which end we also pray always for you," writes
Paul, placing the stress upon the word "you." His present
concern is for his afflicted converts in Thessalonica. His
continual petition for them is, "That our God may count
you worthy of your calling." This "calling" refers to the
divine invitation to follow Christ, and it includes the final
blessedness in which the acceptance of the call will issue.
The phrase, "Worthy of your calling," reechoes the notes
of the preceding thanksgiving: "That ye may be counted
worthy of the kingdom of God."

To this end Paul prays that "with power" God may
fulfill for the Thessalonians "every desire of goodness and
every work of faith." "Every desire of goodness" means
every desire which goodness prompts. "Every work of
faith" denotes every work which faith undertakes. The
prayer is that all these desires may be realized, and that
all these works may be brought to a successful issue.

The ultimate aim of the prayer is, "That the name of
our Lord Jesus may be glorified in you, and ye in him."
A name is that by which one is known. The "name" of
Christ denotes all that Christ has been revealed to be, as
divine Savior, as loving Lord. Paul prays that the real
nature, the true character, the full glory of Christ may be

manifest in the Thessalonians, and that they may attain their highest perfection by their union with Christ.

The answer to such a prayer can come only "according to the grace of our God and the Lord Jesus Christ." From such a divine source alone can glory issue. Only by the grace of God and through Christ can our highest aspirations be achieved.

D. THE ADVENT AND THE MAN OF SIN
Ch. 2:1-12

1 Now we beseech you, brethren, touching the coming of our Lord Jesus Christ, and our gathering together unto him; 2 to the end that ye be not quickly shaken from your mind, nor yet be troubled, either by spirit, or by word, or by epistle as from us, as that the day of the Lord is just at hand; 3 let no man beguile you in any wise: for it will not be, except the falling away come first, and the man of sin be revealed, the son of perdition, 4 he that opposeth and exalteth himself against all that is called God or that is worshipped; so that he sitteth in the temple of God, setting himself forth as God. 5 Remember ye not, that, when I was yet with you, I told you these things? 6 And now ye know that which restraineth, to the end that he may be revealed in his own season. 7 For the mystery of lawlessness doth already work: only there is one that restraineth now, until he be taken out of the way. 8 And then shall be revealed the lawless one, whom the Lord Jesus shall slay with the breath of his mouth, and bring to nought by the manifestation of his coming; 9 even he, whose coming is according to the working of Satan with all power and signs and lying wonders, 10 and with all deceit of unrighteousness for them that perish; because they received not the love of the truth, that they might be saved. 11 And for this cause God sendeth them a working of error, that they should believe a lie: 12 that they all might be judged who believed not the truth, but had pleasure in unrighteousness.

The personal return of Christ has been ever the inspiring and purifying hope of the Christian church. Some-

times this cardinal truth has been forgotten and obscured.
Quite as frequently fantastic theories have brought the doctrine into disrepute.   The most common fallacy is the
attempt to set a time, and particularly to proclaim that the
Lord is immediately to appear.   This was the difficulty
in the Thessalonian church.   Paul had comforted the
Christian converts by the assurance that the Lord was to
return to bring them deliverance and to receive them up
in glory.   His words had been interpreted, and a report
was spread abroad, to the effect that "the day of the Lord"
was "just at hand."   To correct the error and to allay the
excitement and consequent disorder, Paul writes to explain that before the Lord returns there will be first an
apostasy from the faith and the appearance of the "man
of sin," whom Christ will destroy at his coming.

This paragraph from the pen of the apostle is specially
needed in the present day as a test and corrective of much
popular teaching concerning the Advent of Christ.

"Now we beseech you, brethren, touching the coming
of our Lord Jesus Christ, and our gathering together unto
him," writes the apostle, as he begins his exhortation and
definitely declares the purpose of his epistle.   The first
chapter was in substance an introduction.   It consisted of
a salutation, a thanksgiving, and a prayer.   The thanksgiving made reference to "the revelation of the Lord Jesus
from heaven with the angels of his power," but here is the
clear announcement that the theme of the letter is to be
"the coming" of Christ.   This word "coming," which translates the Greek term for "presence," never is used by Paul
to designate the present, unseen, spiritual presence of the
Lord, but always indicates his visible return.   In his First
Epistle, Paul has described this return of Christ.   (I Thess.
4:16-17.)   He has assured his readers of the resurrection
of believers which then would take place and of the un-
ending reunion of living and dead with one another and
with the Lord.   Here he is to dwell on only one phase of
the truth.   He is to write of the time of Christ's coming,

or, more specifically, of the events which would precede and follow.

He states his particular purpose to be "to the end that ye be not quickly shaken from your mind, nor yet be troubled, either by spirit, or by word, or by epistle as from us, as that the day of the Lord is just at hand." The return of Christ is a comforting, purifying hope; it should not be the cause of mental agitation or of nervous excitement. The Thessalonians were in danger of being "shaken" from their minds or driven from their sober sense, like a ship from its moorings. They had fallen into a state of alarm, were "troubled" and disturbed. The occasion of this distress was a false report to the effect that "the day of the Lord" was not only approaching, or near, or even "just at hand," but actually "had set in"; it was "present." The day had dawned and the Lord might appear at "any moment." The origin of this false report had been attributed to Paul. Its authority was some prophetic utterance, some oral teaching, some letter supposed to have come from the apostle.

Of course he had made no such misleading statement, and he now proceeds to correct the error and to quiet the minds of the believers. "Let no man beguile you in any wise"—let no man lead you utterly astray "by spirit, or by word, or by epistle," or in any other way—says the apostle. Christ will not return, his coming—or "Parousia" —will not take place, he will not appear, and we shall not be gathered "together unto him," "except the falling away come first, and the man of sin be revealed."

This apostasy, or "falling away," seems to mean a defection from the Christian faith, out of which, or because of which, the man of sin is developed and revealed, in whom the consummation of the apostasy is found.

However, the apostle gives no explanation of this falling away. He does proceed to describe the man of sin, or the "man of lawlessness," as the title appears in many ancient manuscripts. He is here called "the son of perdition," meaning "one who is lost and ruined and destined to destruction." His impious character is such that he "opposeth and exalteth himself against all that is called God or that is worshipped; so that he sitteth in the temple of God, setting himself forth as God." He actually supersedes all forms of religion and demands divine worship for himself alone.

The modern reader cannot but wish that this description of the man of sin had been continued and made more explicit, but Paul suddenly turns from the future to the present. He reminds the Thessalonians of the oral teaching he had given them concerning these matters. He almost reproves them for allowing false teaching to have shaken them from their sober senses: "Remember ye not, that, when I was yet with you, I told you these things?" They should have known that, while the return of Christ might be near, it could never be regarded as immediate until first the man of sin had appeared.

Furthermore, they knew what was delaying or preventing his appearance: "And now ye know that which restraineth, to the end that he may be revealed in his own season." They knew; we of the present day do not know. The mutual understanding between Paul and his readers made it possible for him to speak in those vague and cryptic terms. The key which they held to the cipher has been lost. We cannot be dogmatic in our solution of the riddle. However, it is evident that some power—"that which restraineth"—or some person—"one that restraineth"—was repressing the full manifestation of evil which was to be evidenced in the man of sin: "For the mystery of lawlessness doth already work: only there is one that restraineth now, until he be taken out of the way."

A "mystery" is something once concealed from man but subsequently revealed by the power of the permission of God. So the principle of lawlessness, already at work in secret, or without its full and final manifestation, is being restrained or held back. When the restraint is removed the man of sin will appear. As Paul declares, "And then shall be revealed the lawless one, whom the Lord Jesus shall slay with the breath of his mouth, and bring to nought by the manifestation of his coming." Thus again Paul turns from the present to the future, and predicts that when Christ appears he will destroy utterly, by the mere "breath of his mouth," the last great embodiment of evil.

This man of sin whom Christ is to destroy Paul further describes as one "whose coming is according to the working of Satan." He is an embodiment not only of human wickedness but also of satanic energy. His coming, or parousia, is contrasted with the glorious Parousia of Christ. It will be accompanied and manifested by "all power and signs and lying wonders, and with all deceit of unrighteousness," that is, with all manner of miracles intended to mislead and every kind of wicked device calculated to deceive.

The delusions are intended "for them that perish," for such as are already on the way to perdition. They are so deceived and are so perishing "because they received not the love of the truth, that they might be saved." They are being treated as they deserve. They would not welcome into their hearts the saving truth concerning Christ. Therefore, they have become the victims of falsehood and deception. They are lost, not because they have not heard or have not understood the gospel, but because they have no love for the truth by which they might be saved. The cause of their ruin is not intellectual but moral. It is on account of their aversion to the truth and their preference for falsehood.

"For this cause God sendeth them a working of error, that they should believe a lie." This will be in accordance with a perfectly natural process. Those who willfully reject Christian truth are punished by becoming the dupes of destructive delusions. The purpose and the result of such delusions is the just condemnation of those who reject the gospel and delight in evil: "That they all might be judged who believed not the truth, but had pleasure in unrighteousness."

Unquestionably this passage (ch. 2:1-12) constitutes

one of the most perplexing paragraphs in the New Testament. Any exposition must be presented with humility and reserve. What is meant by this apostasy, by the man of sin, by the power or person that "restraineth"? Many contradictory lines of interpretation have been attempted. Four of these might be mentioned:

Some modern writers regard the passage as a mere speculation on the part of Paul. If intended as a prediction, it never has been fulfilled and never can be fulfilled. Such a view is inconsistent with a belief in the inspiration and authority of the apostle.

Many interpreters identify the man of sin with some one historic character, such as Nero, or Caligula, or Mohammed, or Napoleon. The obvious objection is that the man of sin is to continue in power until he is destroyed by the personal, visible coming of Christ.

For centuries the orthodox Protestant position was that the pope of Rome, or the papacy, was the man of sin, the restraining power being the Roman Empire and the "temple of God" being the Christian church. This view has been abandoned in recent years, largely because of the fact that the popes do not claim for themselves exclusive divine honors. No pope "is called God" or "worshipped" as God, but each declares himself to be the "vicar" of Christ and only as such infallible in matters of religion.

The most probable view is that Paul had in mind the principle of lawlessness, working in his day, causing distress to the followers of Christ, but restrained by Roman law and power. This evil principle has continued to work and has been embodied in many historic characters. Just before the return of Christ it will have its final manifestation in one supreme person, or movement, or system. The restraining power may be civil law and government. A future apostasy from revealed religion may find its climax in a man of sin, who, defying all law and denouncing all religion, may demand to be worshiped as God.

Whatever interpretation is accepted, it is wise to fix the

thought upon the central ideas of the prophecy, to view these in the light of related Scripture, and to be guarded against confusing the creations of fancy with inspired truth.

It seems evident that the return of Christ is the continual comfort and inspiration and hope of the church in the face of all impiety and persecution and unbelief.

This return should be regarded as possibly near in any generation or lifetime. However, it will not occur until after the man of sin has been revealed. The coming, or parousia, of this embodiment of lawlessness, must precede the coming, or Parousia, of Christ. (Vs. 8-9.) Whatever mysteries confront us, however victorious the forces of evil ever may appear, we can rest assured that to be on the side of Christ is to be on the side of ultimate triumph and of eternal truth.

E. THANKSGIVING, EXHORTATION, AND PRAYER   Ch. 2:13-17

13 But we are bound to give thanks to God always for you, brethren beloved of the Lord, for that God chose you from the beginning unto salvation in sanctification of the Spirit and belief of the truth: 14 whereunto he called you through our gospel, to the obtaining of the glory of our Lord Jesus Christ. 15 So then, brethren, stand fast, and hold the traditions which ye were taught, whether by word, or by epistle of ours.

16 Now our Lord Jesus Christ himself, and God our Father who loved us and gave us eternal comfort and good hope through grace, 17 comfort your hearts and establish them in every good work and word.

From the melancholy picture of the unbelieving, deluded victims of the man of sin, Paul turns with a sigh of relief to give thanks for his converts who are receiving salvation by faith in Christ. So full of meaning are these two brief verses (vs. 13-14) that they have been said to form a "system of theology in miniature." Beginning with the eternal

choice of God, Paul describes the salvation of believers as
wrought out in time by the sanctifying power of the Holy
Spirit and completed as they share the very glory of Christ
in the life to come.

"But we are bound to give thanks . . . always for
you," writes the apostle. Both the "we" and the "you"
are emphatic. Paul feels a deep obligation to God for the
faith and the salvation of his Thessalonian friends. He
addresses them as "brethren beloved of the Lord." They
are brethren beloved by Paul and they are also those whom
Christ loved, and they are the continuing objects of His
love.

Paul declares his gratitude "that God chose" them
"from the beginning unto salvation." Probably this choice
points to the divine love whereby they were chosen "before the foundation of the world" (Eph. 1:4), although
this salvation was made possible by providences which
brought Paul to Thessalonica and gave these readers the
opportunity of hearing the "good news."

This salvation was actually accomplished by the "sanctification of the Spirit." It can be realized only in a re-
newed moral character. No man is "saved" unless he is
transformed by the Spirit of God. However, faith is the
instrument in this spiritual renewal. The salvation of
the Thessalonians was by "belief of the truth." Thus the
experience has its human side as well as its divine. The
eternal choice of God is accompanied by the free choice of
man as he accepts the truth revealed in the gospel and sub-
mits his will to the Lordship of Christ.

So Paul reminds his readers that they have been "called"
to this salvation by the gospel he has proclaimed. The
divine choice became effective through the gospel sum-
mons as it has been sounded forth by Paul and his companions. The purpose and end of this call is "the obtaining
of the glory of our Lord Jesus Christ."

Thus "salvation" as employed by Paul is a large and
comprehensive term. It includes the whole experience of

a Christian.   It begins in a new spiritual birth; it continues through life in a growth and perfecting of moral character; it finds its culmination in heavenly glory and eternal fellowship with Christ.   When Paul contrasts this experience of his converts with the awful fate of those "who believed not the truth, but had pleasure in unrighteousness," it is natural that he should give thanks.   As he attributes this salvation to the divine choice, wrought out by divine power, made effective through a divine message, and perfected in divine glory, it is inevitable that he should give thanks to God and to God alone.

Thanksgiving passes into exhortation.   In fact, the theme of the thanksgiving is the ground of the command: "So then, brethren, stand fast, and hold the traditions which ye were taught, whether by word, or by epistle of ours."   Divine grace does not exclude human effort.   It rather encourages it and assures its ultimate success.   The very fact that the Thessalonians are beloved of Christ, and chosen and called of God to obtain eternal glory, should inspire them to faithful fulfillment of Christian duty in work and word.   The exhortation is rather specific, however, and refers to the particular condition set forth in this entire chapter of the epistle.   Since they know that the coming of the Lord may be near but cannot be immediate, since they are sure of their own safety and salvation, they are encouraged to "stand fast" against all opposition and persecution and false doctrine.   They are not to be agitated, not to be nervously excited, but to hold firmly and calmly the "traditions" which they have been taught by Paul.   These traditions do not refer to any ancient sayings handed down from distant generations, but to the instructions given to the Thessalonians by the apostle.   They include not only his teaching as to the Second Advent but also his entire gospel message.   These had been in the form of oral teaching and of written communication.

Thus, "by word" refers to the instruction given while Paul was with the Thessalonians, and "by epistle of ours"

denotes his first epistle to the Thessalonian church. With
these definite and clear truths in mind, they should not be
disturbed by any false and disquieting prediction purporting to come from Paul, whether in the form of prophetic
utterance or distorted saying or spurious epistle.

It is true that most of the heated discussions and fanati-
cal disturbances and fantastic theories related to the return
of Christ are due, not to the plain teaching of Christ and
his apostles, but to the misinterpretation of Scripture and
to the vagaries of human fancy.

The exhortation is followed by a prayer: "Now our
Lord Jesus Christ himself, and God our Father who loved
us and gave us eternal comfort and good hope through
grace, comfort your hearts and establish them in every
good work and word." Paul realizes that his appeal can
be obeyed and fulfilled only by divine power. It is for
this reason that he offers this petition to Christ the Son
and to God the Father.

The union and the order of the names are almost startling, for to Son and Father equal honor is ascribed, and
indeed the Son is mentioned first. Both are one in their
love to the church and one in their saving work. This
divine love was manifested in the sufferings and death of
Christ, as also in all his mission. Issuing from this love
are the divine gifts of "eternal comfort and good hope."
It is a comfort which gives strength to endure all the trials
of life, to defy death itself, and to rest assured that nothing
can prevent the objects of the divine love from sharing
the future glory of Christ. The hope is good, because it
will never deceive; it is joyous and genuine, blessed in its
present effects, and sure to be realized fully in the life to
come. Both the "eternal comfort" and the "good hope"
are due to the unmerited favor of God. They are "through
grace."

Based on such gracious gifts is the petition for comfort
and strength. In view of such manifestation of love the
apostle is encouraged to pray that the Lord Jesus Christ
and God the Father may "comfort your hearts and estab-

lish them in every good work and word." The comfort
is not merely consolation in sorrow, but also courage for
brave endurance and vigorous action. The petition is also
that the hearts of the readers may be established, or
strengthened, so that as a result they may be steadfast and
strong in every good work that they do and in every good
word that they speak.

F. REQUEST FOR PRAYER AND EXPRESSION OF CONFIDENCE   Ch. 3:1-5

*1 Finally, brethren, pray for us, that the word of the
Lord may run and be glorified, even as also it is with you;
2 and that we may be delivered from unreasonable and
evil men; for all have not faith. 3 But the Lord is faithful,
who shall establish you, and guard you from the evil one.
4 And we have confidence in the Lord touching you, that
ye both do and will do the things which we command. 5
And the Lord direct your hearts into the love of God, and
into the patience of Christ.*

Missionaries and pastors and all other Christian workers
covet and appreciate the prayers of their supporters and
parishioners and personal friends. So, when the apostle
has voiced his prayer for the readers, he turns to ask their
prayers for himself. He introduces the request by the
word "finally." The epistle is drawing to its close. It
has contained valuable instruction; now there is to follow
an important command. The prayer which is requested
is to have two specific objects. The first is, "That the
word of the Lord may run and be glorified." The general
meaning is, "That the gospel may have a triumphant career." More specifically, "may run" possibly indicates a
progress which is not only rapid, but is also unhindered.
"Glorified" may indicate a manifested power of the gospel
in the transformed lives of those by whom it is received.
Such progress and such triumph had attended the preaching of "the word of the Lord" among the Thessalonians.
Therefore Paul adds, "As also it is with you." The praise

thus implied is intended, as indeed the whole paragraph
is intended, to form a tactful introduction to the command
Paul is about to give.

The second object for which the readers are expected to
pray is the deliverance of the apostle: "That we may be
delivered from unreasonable and evil men." These two
objects are closely related. "The word of the Lord" can
"run and be glorified" only as obstacles and opposition
are removed from the path of the apostle. As Paul writes,
however, the opposition is very severe. It is being offered
by men who are not only "unreasonable," but, as this
word implies, are perverse and unrighteous and unjust,
and, as Paul adds, are "evil" or wicked. He probably
had in mind the Jews of Corinth who were attacking and
opposing him with bitter hatred. The reason for their
opposition was their rejection of the gospel, their real
antipathy to the truth of Christ. As Paul says in explanation of their malice, "All have not faith." There are those
for whom the gospel has no affinity, to whom it does not
belong, and by whom it never will be received.

"All have not faith. But the Lord is faithful," writes
Paul, seeming to play upon the words, and turning suddenly from his own trials to those which beset his readers.
He is certain that, however bitter their persecution, however severe their temptations, the Lord in whom they have
trusted will keep them firm and steadfast and will deliver
them from the assaults of "the evil one."

Furthermore, Paul expresses his confidence in his converts. He possibly continues to play upon the thought of
faith. "The Lord is faithful . . . ," he writes. "And we
have confidence in . . . you," trusting in the faithfulness
of the Lord, "that ye both do and will do the things which
we command." These "things" are not the exhortations
which have already been given, but those which immediately follow and which form the substance of this last
chapter of the epistle.

However, in order that the Lord may show his faithfulness and make it possible for the readers truly and gladly to obey, Paul breathes out another brief prayer: "And the Lord direct your hearts into the love of God, and into the patience of Christ." "The love of God" is the love which God has revealed and which he continues to bestow. "The patience of Christ" is the patience, the steadfastness, which Christ manifested and which he inspires and supplies. This is the probable meaning of these phrases. However, some interpret them as meaning "love toward God" and "a patient waiting for the return of Christ." Both interpretations are beautiful and forceful, but the former appears to be the more accurate. The petition is that the Lord may guide the hearts of the believers into a deepening and abiding sense of the love of God and into a fuller experience of the steadfast endurance which Christ alone can provide. Such an experience will enable the readers to obey the command which Paul is about to give. Such an experience will enable us all and always more perfectly to do the will of God.

G. DISCIPLINE OF THE DISORDERLY
Ch. 3:6-15

6 Now we command you, brethren, in the name of our Lord Jesus Christ, that ye withdraw yourselves from every brother that walketh disorderly, and not after the tradition which they received of us. 7 For yourselves know how ye ought to imitate us: for we behaved not ourselves disorderly among you; 8 neither did we eat bread for nought at any man's hand, but in labor and travail, working night and day, that we might not burden any of you: 9 not because we have not the right, but to make ourselves an ensample unto you, that ye should imitate us. 10 For even when we were with you, this we commanded you, If any will not work, neither let him eat. 11 For we hear of some that walk among you disorderly, that work not at all, but are busybodies. 12 Now them that are such we command and exhort in the Lord Jesus Christ, that with quietness

*they work, and eat their own bread. 13 But ye, brethren,
be not weary in well-doing. 14 And if any man obeyeth
not our word by this epistle, note that man, that ye have
no company with him, to the end that he may be ashamed.
15 And yet count him not as an enemy, but admonish him
as a brother.*

Work is a blessing and a boon. Idleness, unless it is
enforced, is attended by danger and disgrace. The example of our Lord in the carpenter shop at Nazareth and
the teaching of his apostles emphasize the dignity of labor
and the nobility of honest toil. In the church at Thessalonica there were those who refused to work and who in-
sisted upon being supported by their fellow Christians.
Probably their idleness was due in large measure to the
prevalent false teaching to the effect that "the day of the
Lord" was "just at hand." Expecting the coming of Christ
to be immediate, they had deserted their daily tasks and in
selfish inaction were waiting to "be caught up in the clouds,
to meet the Lord in the air."

Whether or not this feverish expectancy of the Lord's
return and this idleness on the part of certain Christians
were directly connected, these two topics do occupy the
main portion of the epistle. Paul first has given instruction
as to the time of the Lord's return; he now turns to give
his admonition concerning those Christians who refuse to
work. The situation is evidently serious, and the words of
the apostle are marked by emotion. They are of deep im-
port as to the treatment of all persons who deserve the discipline of the church.

The solemn exhortation is in the name of Christ: "Now
we command you, brethren, in the name of our Lord Jesus
Christ." The phrase means not the mere title of Christ;
the "name" of Christ denotes all that Christ is and all
that he has been revealed to be. In virtue of the fact
that he is our Savior and our Lord and Master, we obey
him and trust him. So Paul gives his "command" with
the authority of an apostle who has been called and em-
powered by Christ.

"Withdraw yourselves from every brother that walketh disorderly" is the command. The word "brother" designates any member of the Thessalonian church. The "disorderly" persons are described in a later sentence as those "that work not at all, but are busybodies." Their lives are not rightly ordered. They seem not to be guilty of actual and intentional wrongdoing, but to be neglecting daily duties and falling into idle and meddlesome habits.

They are definitely described as walking "not after the tradition which they received" of Paul. This "tradition" refers again to the definite oral instruction given to the Thessalonians by Paul during his stay with them. He had taught them how to live orderly and industrious and exemplary lives.

From those who are disorderly and are disregarding Paul's instructions, the other Christians are commanded to "withdraw" themselves. The discipline should consist in an actual or virtual suspension from fellowship. The reasons for demanding such drastic action are then detailed:

First of all, there is the example of the apostle himself. He had proved to be no idler when among them, but had provided a pattern of tireless industry. "For yourselves know how ye ought to imitate us," he writes: "for we behaved not ourselves disorderly among you; neither did we eat bread for nought at any man's hand." Paul emphasizes this course of manly independence by two considerations: There was the burdensome, exhausting nature of his work. It was wearisome toil; it involved hardship. Far into the night he labored, after days of preaching and teaching. He plied his trade as a tentmaker so that he might not place a financial burden on his converts.

Then, furthermore, his manual labor was the more notable because he realized that it was not necessary. He knew that he had the right to be supported by his converts. It was the teaching of his Master and his own deep conviction that those who preach the gospel have the "right to receive remuneration for their labor. However, he waived that right to strengthen the force of his example. "Not because we have not the right," Paul insists, "but to make ourselves an ensample unto you, that ye should imitate us."

The second reason for demanding discipline for the disorderly is the specific teaching of the apostle when in Thessalonica: "For even when we were with you, this we commanded you, If any will not work, neither let him eat." It is to be noticed that Paul does not make the obvious remark, "If anyone does not work, he will have nothing to eat," or, "If anyone does not work, he will deserve nothing to eat." Paul issues a command: "If any man refuses to work, if he is unwilling to work, he shall not eat."

The third reason for his requiring discipline in the Thessalonian church is the seriousness of the situation as reported to him: "For we hear of some that walk among you disorderly." This disorderly conduct is defined. They "work not at all, but are busybodies." The play upon words in the original Greek may be indicated in English by, "Doing no business but being busybodies," or "Busy only with what is not their own business." These persons Paul solemnly enjoins to resume their occupation and their self-support: "Now them that are such we command and exhort in the Lord Jesus Christ, that with quietness they work, and eat their own bread."

After this rebuke of the idle and meddlesome disturbers of the church, Paul turns to address again the loyal and orderly members who form the main body of his readers: "But ye, brethren, be not weary in well-doing." No matter what may be the conduct of others, do not fail in doing the fair and noble thing. Persevere in your honorable course. Do not tire in the path of duty.

In spite of his explicit command and exhortation previously addressed to the idle and disturbing element, Paul realizes that some may continue in their wrong course. He therefore insists that such persons must be disciplined by the church: "If any man obeyeth not our word by this

epistle, note that man, that ye have no company with him."
Disobedience to authority, disorderly conduct in the church
cannot be regarded with indifference. The character of the
Christian community must be maintained. The idle and
meddlesome members must be deprived of all association
and fellowship with the other members of the brotherhood.
For more serious offenses, more severe penalties were enjoined by Christ (Matt. 18:15-17) and elsewhere by Paul
(I Cor. 5:5).

However, no matter how flagrant the fault, the real purpose of discipline is the reclamation of the offender. It is
"to the end that he may be ashamed." Furthermore, no
matter how severe the penalty, the spirit with which it is
imposed must be a spirit of pity and of charity: "Yet
count him not as an enemy, but admonish him as a
brother."

For all that Paul has been urging in this paragraph, a
divine example is found in the conduct of our Lord. He
gave encouragement in honest toil as he labored in the
shop at Nazareth. He severely rebuked sin and insincerity
in those who claimed to be the religious leaders of the day.
Yet to the most notorious sinners he showed sympathy
and love; he pronounced pardon; he bade them go in
peace.

H. CONCLUSION   Ch. 3:16-18

*16 Now the Lord of peace himself give you peace at all
times in all ways. The Lord be with you all.*

*17 The salutation of me Paul with mine own hand,
which is the token in every epistle: so I write. 18 The
grace of our Lord Jesus Christ be with you all.*

This rather tempestuous epistle comes to a peaceful
close. It is like a golden sunset after a day of storm. The
opening chapter is lurid with "flaming fire," "vengeance,"
and "eternal destruction." The second chapter deals with

the impious, satanic man of sin, "whom the Lord Jesus shall slay with the breath of his mouth." The last chapter concerns the discipline of disorderly members of the church. Yet amid all the tumult of emotion there are periods of calm in the epistle. Again and again is heard the gentle voice of prayer. So here, as the letter concludes, Paul offers his petition for peace: "Now the Lord of peace himself give you peace at all times."

The reference may be to "the God of peace." More probably it is to Christ, who, amid all opposition and outrage, maintained an unbroken tranquillity of soul. He gave peace as his legacy to his disciples: "Peace I leave with you; my peace I give unto you." He is still the Source of peace to his followers. Through him they "have peace with God"; by his grace they can maintain peace with one another; and his Spirit can breathe into their hearts a peace which is unbroken through all the trials and temptations and distresses of life. Paul prays that such peace may be granted to his readers "at all times in all ways."

Then he adds, "The Lord be with you all." This abiding presence had been promised to his followers by the Lord himself. Paul would have his readers believe in that presence and so yield themselves to the will of the Master that his peace and his power may be manifest in their lives. The prayer is for "all"—for those distressed by the death of friends, for those disturbed by the predicted return of Christ, for those whose conduct requires the discipline of the church. A living and present Lord can meet the need of all who look to him for help.

At this point Paul seems to take the pen from the scribe to whom he has been dictating the epistle. In his own handwriting he composes the concluding verses. He says in effect: "And now with my own hand I add this closing greeting, signing it with my name, Paul. This I am in the habit of doing. It is a mark of genuineness in all my letters. This is my own signature." Such an ending gives a

graphic touch and a note of reality to the epistle. It intimates, probably, that Paul had a much larger correspon-
dence than we now possess and possibly hints at a danger
of forged letters even at this early date. It must indicate,
further, Paul's sense of authority and his conviction of the
correctness of his teaching and of the importance of the
messages which this letter contains.

The final benediction which the apostle thus pens with
his own hand is in the familiar form: "The grace of our
Lord Jesus Christ be with you all." The very word
"grace" might be regarded as a proof that the epistle came
from Paul, even had he not penned these words in his dis-
tinctive handwriting; for "grace" is Paul's distinguishing
and favorite term. His salutation at the opening of his
letters and his benedictions at their close center largely in
this luminous, melodious word. It is for Paul the beginning and the end of the gospel. That unmerited love
which brought Christ into the world as our Savior to suffer and die and rise again for our redemption, that grace
whereby we are reconciled to God and made fit to be par-
takers of his glory, that grace which is ever offered to us
will be sufficient for all our needs, as we seek for ever-
fresh supplies from "our Lord Jesus Christ." To him be
all the glory both now and evermore. Amen.